THE BATTLE OF BRITAIN

The Home Front

by

George Goldsmith-Carter

Mason & Lipscomb PUBLISHERS   NEW YORK

Library of Congress Catalog Card Number: 74-4305

International Standard Book Number: 0-88405-073-4

First Printing

Printed in the United States of America

Library of Congress Cataloging in Publication Data

Goldsmith-Carter, George.
   The battle of Britain; the home front.

   SUMMARY: Describes Germany's long siege of Britain emphasizing
the effects on British citizens.
   Bibliography: p.
   1. World War, 1939-1945—Great Britain. 2. Britain, Battle of, 1940.
[1. World War, 1939-1945—Great Britain. 2. Britain, Battle of, 1940]
I. Title.
D759.C286   940.53'42   74-4305
ISBN 0-88405:073-4

Contents

List of Illustrations

Introduction

ONE OF MY MOST vivid, exciting, and terrible memories is that of sitting as a child at my bedroom window in the East End of London and breathlessly watching a night-raiding Zeppelin caught in a cone of searchlights during World War I.

Above the great hovering, silver-colored, cigar-shaped airship, the tiny, mothlike shape of a primitive biplane swooped down like a striking hawk and spat slim twin streams of flaming incendiary bullets into the vast airship.

The envelope of the airship glowed red where the bullets had pierced it and from the glowing patch leaped a fan-shaped tongue of flame, which flashed into a roaring furnace as the hydrogen gas in the mighty envelope ignited.

Sagging more and more terribly in the middle, the great airship, now a raging inferno, the engines roaring frightfully, sank lower and lower. I crouched there terrified with my frightened mother, watching the burning bodies of the crew falling from the skies like tiny shooting stars.

Eventually, the Zeppelin—all that was left of it—crashed at a place called Cuffley in the county of Essex. Its crew perished to a man, some leaping to death, others being incinerated in the flying holocaust.

A milkman at work early in the morning found the body of the Zeppelin's commander, and so a legend was born. It is said that the German commander was a giant, seven feet tall and that the buttons of his uniform were of solid gold.

The huge, slow, gas-filled Zeppelins proved to be too vulnerable; and after several of them had been destroyed, the Germans commenced to bombard London with squadrons of twin-engine Gotha bombers.

On one such day raid on London, my father and mother, concerned with the safety of relatives, took me to Poplar, a place deep in the heart of London's East End, which had taken the brunt of the bombing. Here I witnessed the second and most terrible of my childhood memories.

A crude bomb, so small that it had been dropped by hand, had left a little hole in the roof of a big school and had crashed through several floors to explode on the ground floor, where the youngest children were being taught.

Clasping my father's hand, I saw the bodies of small children being carried out by rescuers and dust-covered, shocked, and weeping teachers. Suddenly, my father swung me away from the sight, but he was too late to prevent my seeing the awful imprint of a slain child on the white dress of a tiny girl who was being led out of the wrecked classroom, walking as if in a dream.

That murdered child was one of the 1,413 victims of

the German Zeppelins and Gotha bombers that raided London during World War I.

I did not know then that I was seeing history in the making in the killing of these innocents, for London was the first city in history to be bombarded by aircraft. I could not know then that within 30 years the bombers of the Nazi Luftwaffe would bring more death and destruction to London in a single night than the Zeppelins and Gothas of World War I had wrought in 100 raids.

GEORGE GOLDSMITH-CARTER

The Battle of Britain

1. Britain Prepares for War

In the spring of 1938, Adolf Hitler, leader of the Nazi party in Germany, annexed Austria on the pretext of uniting his country with the German-speaking people of Austria. His next objective was Czechoslovakia, and he used as an excuse the liberation of the German-speaking areas of this country.

On September 15 of the same year, Neville Chamberlain, the British prime minister, flew to Germany for peace talks with Hitler on this matter. They had further talks on September 22, this time at Godesberg, where Hitler made it very plain that he was dissatisfied with the slow progress of Britain and France (who had been Czechoslovakia's allies since 1924) in agreeing to his demands. The situation between Britain and Germany was now so tense that on September 25 a British organization known as the Air Raid Precaution was mobilized and balloon barrages appeared over London.

On September 28, as Chamberlain was discussing his peace plans in the House of Commons, he received a direct message from Hitler inviting him to Munich for further talks about Czechoslovakia. So peremptory was the message that the House of Commons was thrown into an uproar; and while Chamberlain was flying to Germany, the British government made hasty plans to evacuate two million citizens from London. Thirty-eight million gas masks were also swiftly issued to the public. For it was plain that Germany's powerful air force would strike first at London.

Anticlimax followed hard on the heels of Chamberlain's alarm. When the air raid sirens sounded an alert in London, the "invader" proved to be only a French aircraft passing innocently over; but two groups of British combat planes had taken off to engage the "enemy." Owing to an error, they engaged each other over the lower reaches of the Thames. Two planes were shot down; and one pilot killed in what became known, with bitter irony, as the Battle of Barking Creek.

While the French and Germans watched each other from behind the massive concrete fortifications of the Maginot and the Siegfried lines, Britain began to evacuate its children from cities and towns to safe places in the countryside. In fact, as early as June, 1939, when war was obviously inevitable, British people had begun to move away from densely populated areas, knowing from the experience of World War I that bombardment from the air must come. Something like 3¾ million people were evacuated, and one of the first minor tragedies of the war was the wholesale destruction of family pets that could not go with their owners.

At the beginning of the war, the British government evolved two official evacuation plans: the Yellow Plan and the Black Plan. Under the Yellow Plan, most government departments were to leave for safer parts of the country.

Thus about 25,000 civil servants left London to set up their offices and departments in large seaside hotels and boardinghouses, whose owners were officially dispossessed. Unfortunately, the Yellow Plan did not work, and chaos ensued. For several weeks after war had been declared, the requisitioned hotels and boardinghouses remained empty, to the loud and righteous indignation of the ousted owners and the national daily press, which supported them.

Black Plan, designed to evacuate the entire government from London if the city were heavily attacked, was abandoned altogether when it became obvious that no part of the entire country would be safe from enemy air attack.

In the meantime, the British Broadcasting Corporation established itself in a large country mansion at Evesham in Worcestershire. The Bank of England was moved to a little village called Overton in Hampshire, and the priceless pictures in London's National Gallery were carefully packed and hidden in a remote cave in North Wales.

Everyone's concern was to get as far away as possible from cities, towns, and heavily populated areas, where enemy bombs would fall. There were two types of evacuation, private and official.

In the case of private evacuation, some two million people left cities and towns at their own expense for hamlets and villages and the wide open spaces in the north of Scotland; the mountainous country of Wales; the wide moorlands of southwest England; and the small villages and country towns of east, south, and southwest England generally. Several thousand people felt that even these places were not far enough away from German bombers and so departed for America.

This private exodus of those wealthy enough to go

without assistance from the state was a relatively simple matter, but the official evacuation was an entirely different and vastly more complex business, for it meant the billeting of millions of working-class people from towns on all classes and types of people who lived in the country. It involved house-to-house checking all over Britain by volunteers to establish how much room was available for the evacuees.

The evacuation of children from London. *Courtesy of London Transport Board*

The evacuation of school children to places of safety was the main task, and the results were unexpected and far from satisfactory. Less than half of London's school children left the city for a variety of reasons, whereas in the industrial areas of the densely populated Midlands and northern counties, only about a quarter of the children left. On the other hand, about two-thirds of the school children of Lancashire's teeming towns and cities were taken to safer places.

The average evacuation of children in England was 48 percent; but in Scotland, only 37 percent. Scotland, generally speaking, is less industrialized than England and therefore lacks the same density of population.

The words *official evacuation* create the picture of children being bundled up like parcels and sent wherever they had to go, but it was not that simple. Truly like parcels, the children had labels telling who they were and to which destination they had to go. Some wore armlets, and groups carried placards. Getting to those destinations, however, was another thing entirely.

In three days something like a million and a half children, teachers, mothers with babies, expectant mothers, cripples, and blind people left the towns and cities, clutching gas mask cases, suitcases, parcels of clothing, and emergency rations for their journeys. Up to this point, the organization was good, but the traveling conditions were often appalling and the arrivals chaotic.

Mothers and children from towns, who were used to such things as indoor flush toilets and tap water, were sent to remote, primitive farm cottages, where the only toilet was an "earth lavatory"—a large iron bucket topped by a board with a hole in it—sited in a wooden shack some distance from the house. For water they had to rely on wells and pumps, also out of doors in most cases. The water in some instances should have been declared undrinkable. Although the locals who drank it had become immune to the bacteria it contained, it caused dysentery-type maladies in those not used to it.

There are many places in the ancient rural parts of Britain so lonely and with such an inexplicably hostile atmosphere that even the countryfolk avoid them after dark. It is easy to understand, therefore, that children from densely populated cities were terrified and bewildered by the empty and somehow threatening silence of such places as many of them had never seen or even dreamed existed. To these town and city children, especially after dark, the quiet fields, the lonely moors and mountains, the dark woods and forests were the homes of ghosts, goblins, and monsters. When night fell, they would not go outside the door, even when nature urged a visit to the lavatory.

From this mass evacuation of town children to rural areas a surprising fact emerged. The wealthy and sophisticated people were less troubled by the uproar and by the habits of their young charges than the middle classes were. And the middle classes were less troubled than the simple, unsophisticated country folk. Some of the habits of the children, especially those from slum areas, would have shattered the serenity of an Indian Yogi, for between 5 and 10 percent of the children evacuated had never been taught basic hygiene, and some of them thought nothing of using whatever room they happened to be in as a lavatory.

Clothing was another problem. Vast numbers of children from poor homes arrived at their new abodes nearly in rags and with no change of clothing. Some of the parents of these children were so poor that they could not buy their children a second shift of clothing, and others were indifferent to the plight of their offspring. As a result, many of the foster-parents bought clothing for the children at their own expense. Charitable committees also raised funds for this purpose, and the government supplied money to local educational authorities in the evacuation zones to use as and when they thought necessary.

The picture of the exacuation of Britain's children was far from being entirely an unhappy one, however. In many instances, the lively youngsters from the busy towns brought a new lease of life to the old and lonely people who gave them homes, and many of the town children took to country life as ducks take to water. Pale and thin-limbed children from the slums began to show marked improvement in health and physique, thanks to plenty of clean air and a wholesome diet. In a number of cases, these town and city-bred youngsters eventually came to love their foster-parents better than their real parents, and some learned to love their new environment so much that they stayed on to grow up and become country folk themselves when the war was over.

Yet this first evacuation of the children proved to be an overall failure, owing to the fact that up to that moment the towns and cities of Britain had not been bombed, and many of the children and their mothers drifted back to the densely populated areas. Many of the mothers missed the bright lights, the cinemas, the public houses, taverns, and dance halls of the towns and cities and worried about the welfare of their husbands, who had been left behind to do their various jobs. Thus it was that tens of thousands of mothers went back to the densely populated areas, leaving their children behind.

Lack of money caused whole families to return to city life. Out-of-work fathers with nothing but unemployment benefits and social security allowances to live on could send little if any money to their families who had been evacuated to the country. It was easier for poor people to live together in poverty than for them to live apart in poverty.

Nor, at the beginning of the war, was the financial position of the majority of the foster-parents and guardians of evacuated children a happy one. Those who provided homes for the children received only ten shillings and six-pence weekly (about $1.50 then) for the first child and eight shillings and sixpence weekly (or about $1.20 then) for every child they looked after beyond the first. These sums had to cover full board and lodging.

For mothers with babies or very small children, those who billeted them received five shillings for the mother and three shillings for each child weekly. As these sums were for lodging only, the evacuated mothers had to buy and cook food for themselves and their children.

The evacuation of the children caused many other problems when it came to schooling. One reason was that there was nothing like enough school accommodation for the large numbers of children who had been evacuated to the country. Tens of thousands of children with their teachers plodded around the lanes and byways of the countryside, searching for suitable buildings in which to set up schools. They settled in church halls, assembly halls, village halls, peacetime holiday camps, dance halls, empty ambulance stations, and even in derelict buildings. In instances where entire schools and teachers had been evacuated, they shared the school of the village or town to which they had been sent, the teachers working on a shift system.

The chaos was made even worse by the fact that any

empty buildings available were quickly requisitioned for other purposes. The Civil Defence Organisation alone had already taken over something like 2,000 schools in Britain. Two-thirds of London's school buildings were taken over by such groups as well as something like two thirds of those of the city of Manchester, to give just two examples. Because of this, teachers were forced to hold classes in the homes of the children's parents or foster-parents or, failing this, in social welfare centers when they could. In many instances, classes could be held only for one hour a day, and the teachers then had to devise enough homework to fill the remaining time.

Some good came from this, however, for when the children eventually settled down to this strange way of learning, the town children learned a good deal about country life from their new schoolmates and the country children learned much about town life from the evacuees. In this way, their mutual education was furthered in a manner that could not have occurred in peacetime.

All this strange and unique upheaval of war put a heavy burden on teachers; for when the hard day was over, they had to take groups of small, frightened town children home through dark and muddy lanes and byways, where street lighting and transport did not exist. In addition, the teachers had to devise ways of keeping the more adventurous town children out of mischief after school hours. It was easy to *tell* lively town and city-bred youngsters, who had never lived in the country, that the gates of fields and pastures had to be kept shut to keep farm animals from straying; but it was a great deal more taxing to see that they did it.

All children love making campfires, but it was difficult

to ensure that town-bred children did not make their fires in farm stackyards, where valuable hay and grain could be destroyed or where forest fires could easily destroy thousands of trees. A group of tough youngsters from London's East End might think that "rodeo" with a field full of pedigree dairy cows was fun, but the farmer who owned the cows had other ideas. And so frictions were born.

In the meantime, the million or so children who had gone back to the towns and cities that had so far remained safe from enemy bombers, found their schools closed. Without supervision, they caused the authorities a mountain of problems. Some children, who had been abandoned by heartless or feckless parents, banded into groups that terrorized entire neighborhoods, living on what they could pilfer and sleeping in any deserted house or shack they could find.

Such chaos could not be allowed to continue; so at the beginning of November, 1939, the British government, with Prime Minister Neville Chamberlain still at its head, decreed that where possible, the closed schools in Britain's less crowded and vulnerable areas should be reopened. Obviously, the plans for the evacuation of Britain's children from the dangers of air attack were only partially successful.

During the Munich crisis just before the outbreak of the war, something like half a million people had joined Britain's Air Raid Precaution, called, for convenience, the ARP. In every town and city of Britain, ARP wardens' posts sprang up almost overnight. These posts were heavily sandbagged, concrete blockhouses, about ten feet square and manned by steel-helmeted air raid wardens, who, to begin with at least, were as unpopular with the British public as the British traffic warden is today. The reason for this unpopularity was that the duties of the air raid wardens interfered with the hitherto inviolate liberties of the individual, who was now subjected to a number of new and tedious laws.

A poster of 1942; in the blackout. *Courtesy of London Transport Board*

For example, an air raid warden had the power to reprimand anyone who did not carry his gas mask, an offense punishable by law. Air raid wardens also had the power to reprimand and report to the authorities those who broke the blackout rules by lighting cigarettes or turning on flashlights in the blacked out streets after dark. They also had the power to deal with those who left lights on in houses or buildings and did not cover the windows and doors with blackout curtains or screens. These offenses were also punishable by heavy fines.

The blackout was, apart from the actual bombing itself, the greatest wartime misery and inconvenience the British public endured. The blacking out of a house or premises was a boring and complicated business, although simple enough for those who could afford the expense of heavy blackout curtains for their windows and doors. Blacking out for the average man meant the tedious business of pinning up large sheets of black or brown paper with thumbtacks at night and the equally tedious business of taking them down in the morning. There was also the indignity of being loudly bawled out by air raid wardens or police if so much as a brief or accidental flash of light showed from a window or door after dusk had fallen.

The blackout regulations were directly responsible for the first British civilian casualties of World War II. With street lighting forbidden and automobile headlamps limited to the merest glimmer through specially slotted hoods, the road accidents in the latter half of 1939 were twice as many as in the corresponding period for the previous year and continued at a high rate until gasoline rationing eventually took many automobiles and trucks off the roads.

There were other kinds of accidents too; people fell

down steps, off curbs, off unlit railway station platforms under trains. They fell into canals and rivers; some drowned. They walked painfully into trees, walls, and piles of sandbags; into lampposts, telegraph poles, and into each other. To aggravate the situation, the crime rate soared. There was also the tedium of digging deep holes in gardens to sink the curved steel sections of the Anderson air raid shelters supplied to individual householders for their families, and of erecting steel Morrison air raid shelters indoors. In addition, the glass of all windows had to be made blastproof by sticking lines of tape vertically and horizontally across all windowpanes.

At a time of national uncertainty, one thing *was* certain. The entire British public was becoming thoroughly irritated and bored by the whole dreary and, up till then, unnecessary business. Naturally, the frustrated wrath of the public had to fall on somebody; and it fell heavily on air raid wardens, police, gas decontamination squads, the fire services (whose members were sneered at as draft dodgers), and on civil defense workers generally. It did not help the angry public to see civil defense workers playing "silly games" by staging mock air raid incidents in the street, when passersby were dragged in to play the parts of "casualties" and swathed in artificially bloodstained bandages.

At the same time, public transport was in chaos. Buses and coaches were slow, infrequent, and never on time. Darkened trains, pulling in at dimly lit railway stations, where the station names had been removed to confuse enemy paratroopers when they came, were slow, overcrowded, cold in winter, and devoid of buffet (dining) cars, where bored travelers could have passed the time eating and drinking.

In spite of everything, the civil defense machinery ground slowly and ponderously on. The red tops of all the General Post Office postboxes were painted with a sickly looking, greenish yellow paint, which, in the event of a gas attack, would change color and so warn the gas decontamination squads. Local "gas identification" groups were organized; and the public, already irritated by the gas masks they were forced to carry on pain of fines, was subjected to boring lectures on how to identify a multitude of war gases by smell.

Under the delusion that they were less frightening than the masks issued to adults, children were provided with red rubber "Mickey Mouse" gas masks with chrome-plated eyepieces. Nurses, mothers, and those responsible for the safety of small babies were given rubber, airtight containers with clear plastic windows into which the babies were to be bundled during a gas attack and kept breathing by means of a concertinalike air pump. Fortunately, on all counts, gas attacks from the air never materialized!

Britain's towns, cities, and ports were now protected from low-level bombing by great fleets of silvery barrage balloons, tethered to 400 feet of wire, which sang eerily in the wind.

The British public, although preoccupied with the blackout and civil defense operations, still had time to dwell gloomily on the fact that the enemy, although he had not as yet sent his bombers, had struck three savage blows in the war at sea.

On the very day that war was declared, the outward-bound passenger ship *Athenia* was torpedoed and sunk by a Nazi submarine, with great loss of life, that included many children. On October 14, 1939, another enemy submarine had daringly thrust its way into Britain's naval base at Scapa Flow in the Orkney Islands to torpedo and sink the battleship H.M.S. *Royal Oak* as she lay at anchor. On October 14, German bombers had attacked British naval cruisers lying in the Firth of Forth, Scotland, and killed twenty-five sailors. The morale of the British was not helped much by the Royal Air Forces dropping thousands of propaganda leaflets on Germany.

The truth was that the Chamberlain Government did not really want to fight Germany, but—using World War I tactics—hoped to starve Germany into submission by blockade.

It was a vain hope.

2. Britain Organizes
Her Resources

GERMANY WAS NOT to be intimidated by such feeble gestures as the dropping of propaganda leaflets and threats of blockade. It was now necessary for the British government to take a firm grip on industry and manpower and thrust them in a single direction—that of winning the war by force of arms.

The first thing to be done was to produce vast quantities of bombers and combat planes, guns, tanks, weapons, and munitions of all kinds; but the factories could not be filled with workers at the expense of the armed forces.

To begin with, it was planned that the British Commonwealth of Nations should provide 55 divisions of fighting men. The next priority was ships; for with still vivid memories of the shipping losses to German submarines in World War I, the government knew that such losses, especially of merchant ships carrying food and raw materials, would be great. Thus it was decided that shipbuilding should be doubled at once.

Britain, being a small, densely populated country and

also an island, had always had to rely on importing large quantities of food. This food came by sea from the United States, Canada, Australia, New Zealand, Europe, Scandinavia, Ireland, and other countries. As in World War I, Britain's food ships would now be a major target for German submarines and surface raiders. British ships would also have to face hazards that did not exist in World War I: long-range enemy bombers and acoustic and magnetic mines of enormous destructive power. Obviously, to offset the foreseeable losses, food production would have to be increased as much and as soon as possible. Thus it was planned to plow up an extra two million acres of land to produce more root and grain crops. The British public was exhorted by posters and other means of propaganda to "dig for victory"; to grow vegetables instead of flowers in their gardens; to dig up the lawns, still mowed with ritual reverence each weekend; and to grow potatoes instead of grass.

County War Agricultural Executive Committees were formed to ensure that farms were worked to maximum production; but as the war progressed, many farmers began to hate the officials of the CWAEC almost as much as they hated the Nazis. The farmers accused these officials of bullying, petty feuding, jobbery and favoritism, saying they "multiplied like rabbits, spent money like water, wasted petrol [gasoline] (an increasingly precious commodity brought perilously overseas in tankers, which could erupt into gigantic funeral pyres for their crews), rendered no profit and loss account, were a curse to the farming community, a drain on the nation's economy and exercised unlimited powers." It was a harsh and uncompromising indictment.

The CWAECs also had the power to evict farmers

who got less than 60 percent maximum production from their land. As a result, the CWAEC commandeered something like 400,000 acres of land in England and Wales. The evictions were largely those of nonresident farmers, subtenants who only worked parts of farms and those who worked land that before the war had not been farmland. In about 10 percent of the eviction cases recorded, farmers were forced to leave their farms, which were then taken over by other farmers or by the CWAECs.

Looked at in retrospect, these evictions were sad but understandable, for Britain was to need every ounce of food she could produce. Nevertheless, these dispossessions left British farmers with bitter memories.

In 1940 a Hampshire farmer named Waldron was ordered by the CWAEC to plow up four acres of grassland for crops. He refused to obey and was ordered to quit his farm. This he also refused to do; barricading himself in his farmhouse, he fired on police who had come to evict him, wounding a number of officers with his shotgun. The police then used tear gas but without success. At last, they broke into the farmhouse, where Waldron still continued to fight and at last was shot.

A body known as the Farmers' Rights Association, which had been organized to deal with the complaints of the evicted, declared that Waldron was a martyr to civil rights. Whether Waldron was a martyr or just an obdurate man is debatable, but the tragic and untoward incident became another minor legend of the war.

Farmers also complained with some justification that only 2 percent of Britain's entire steel output had been allocated for the making of agricultural machinery. For plowing up the extra two million acres envisaged, this was totally inadequate. Under these circumstances, the exhortations to farmers to increase vastly their efficiency and production, which came from John Strachey, then minister of food and agriculture, were not well received.

While the might of Nazi Germany was poised to strike a devastating blow at Britain, the country was in a state of internal chaos. The Chamberlain Government, with memories of the bitter industrial strife and unrest of World War I and the 1920s, was frankly afraid of the trade unions, who in turn distrusted Chamberlain's Conservative Government.

The government tried to appease the workers and their trade unions by wage increases coupled with an unsuccessful appeal for voluntary restraint in personal spending to help the war effort. This appeal could hardly have been expected to be heeded by the workers when the government had already passed what was called the Control of Employment Act without any reference at all to the increasingly militant Trade Union movement. This act was intended to make the best use of skilled workers in war industry; they were to be hired either through employment exchanges or through trade unions. But so complicated was the working of the act that it proved to be useless in practice.

Wages were soaring at this time, and skilled workers were being bribed by management to leave factories making war equipment and to go to factories that were still making peacetime luxury and consumer goods.

Nevertheless, in spite of all this confusion, like a steamroller trundling downhill, Britain's war industry slowly gathered power and momentum.

The shipbuilding yards of the Rivers Tyne and Clyde were absorbing the unemployed by building more and more ships. Aircraft factories, arms and munition factories, and motor and machine tool factories were humming; and the textile mills of Lancashire were turning out vast quantities of cloth for uniforms for service men and women.

Since 1938 British industry had been governed by the Schedule of Reserved Occupations, a measure of control introduced when war with Germany first threatened. The object of this schedule was to prevent the drift into the armed forces of skilled workers whose abilities would be of greater use in factories than in the fighting forces.

Regrettably, there was much public scorn and bitterness directed at men who were in reserved occupations. They were called draft dodgers, cowards, and shirkers. One or two were even publicly given a white feather, which in Britain is the symbol for cowardice.

The blitz, so soon to come, was to destroy this stupid attitude forever; for the hurricane of high explosive and incendiary bombs was to show that civilians, whatever their occupation, were very much in the front line of the battle.

As in World War I, World War II inevitably produced a number of conscientious objectors. In the First World War these had been social outcasts, publicly scorned and abused by civilians and even subjected to mental and physical torture when drafted against their will into the armed forces. At the beginning of World War II, Prime Minister Chamberlain declared that there would be no persecution of those who sincerely opposed war. The attitude of the public and of the authorities had become much more tolerant. This was largely due to the fact that the persecution of C.O.'s during World War I had welded them into a group whose pacifist views had spread considerably; there were, in fact, a number of pacifist members of Parliament in the Chamberlain Government.

Conscientious objectors could claim exemption from the armed forces on either pacifist or political grounds. C.O.'s were now interviewed by tribunals that gave complete exemption to those whom they considered sincere. To others, exemption from service in the armed forces was given on the proviso that they agreed to be directed into an approved job. These jobs were usually agricultural, although a number of C.O.'s were directed into the coal mines.

As the various groups were called up for service in the armed forces, it was noticed that the numbers of C.O.'s was diminishing. The pacifist views held in the 1930s were beginning to dwindle before the harsh reality—that Britain was engulfed in a war of survival. Fenner Brockway, a notable pacifist of World War I, stated that although he was still antiwar in outlook, he was also too much aware of the evils of Nazism and Fascism to be completely pacifist.

Nevertheless, during the summer of 1940, when Britain stood in imminent peril of invasion, the general attitude towards C.O.'s hardened considerably. Employers sacked employees known to be C.O.'s, and a considerable number of local authorities also joined in the witch-hunt. Some decided that all employees known to be C.O.'s should be suspended for the duration of the war, while others declared their intention to reduce the wages of the C.O.'s to the same rate as that of a private soldier.

It was at this time that Winston Churchill made a stand in support of the country's conscientious objectors, declaring that any form of persecution, victimization or man hunting was "odious to the British People."

Altogether nearly 60,000 people registered as conscientious objectors, and of these fewer than 4,000 were given unconditional exemption from service in the fighting forces. Nearly 29,000 were registered as C.O.'s on the condition that they agreed to be directed into approved work, mostly on farms or in horticulture. An additional 15,000 did noncombatant work in the armed forces, while just over 12,000 were rejected as C.O.'s altogether. A number of the latter were imprisoned when they refused to obey the authorities, although only about 3 percent of these were jailed as compared to 33 percent during World War I.

Toward the end of September, 1939, Sir John Simon, then chancellor of the exchequer, introduced the first financial budget of the war. It was not an effective one, for, with the terrible and immeasurable cost of a war of survival to be paid, income tax was raised only from five shillings in the pound to seven and sixpence. Moreover, the morale of the working people was not helped by the fact that beer, tobacco, and sugar were also taxed further.

Prices continued to spiral upward. To counter this, the Chamberlain Government introduced a measure that was intended to be temporary, but that was to remain and to prove itself a help in winning the war.

In November, 1939, the Ministry of Food declared that it would be necessary to increase the controlled prices of staple foods. To have done so at this critical period would have proved dangerous to the morale of the entire nation, and not least among the dangers would have been an immediate demand for increased wages from all the trade unions. To avert these dangers and to mollify the trade unions, the government adopted the wise measure of subsidizing the nation's staple foods to the extent of £60 million a year.

In the meantime, food rationing for the entire nation was now imminent. Food ration books had been in existence since 1938, although they had not been issued to the public.

Towards the end of November, 1939, the government announced that from January 8, 1940, food would be rationed. Bacon and ham would be limited to four ounces per person per week, as would butter. Sugar would be rationed to 12 ounces; and meat, to 11 pennyworth per week for each child up to six years old. All people above that age would receive one shilling and tenpence (under 50 cents) worth per week.

Kidneys, liver, hearts, brains, sweetbreads, and so forth would not be rationed. This led to a great deal of bitterness among housewives, for although the majority of butchers were very fair about the distribution of this unrationed meat, others kept it "under the counter" for those who could pay the highest prices. Poultry and rabbits too remained unrationed and, as a result, disappeared from the shops, presumably to be sold to those who could afford fancy prices.

Poultry, rabbits, and pork being very hard to come by, groups of enterprising friends and neighbors acquired these and kept them on a cooperative share system. It was not uncommon for a small group of people to own one pig, having "shares" in the animal (which was very often kept in a small sty at the bottom of somebody's garden). The slaughtering of stock without a government license was strictly forbidden under heavy penalty. But for all this, especially at Christmastime, many a pig was secretly slaughtered in the dead of night, each "shareholder" creeping stealthily off with his allotted portion.

Pork in wartime Britain was worth its weight in gold, and often money could not buy it. The owner of an entire pig could literally dictate his own terms, and bartering pork for valuables other than money was by no means uncommon. In one instance, the owner of a fine antique rifle exchanged the rare weapon for half a pig.

At the beginning of the war, food was still relatively plentiful in Britain; but with the nation's food-carrying ships already under attack from German submarines and aircraft and with the aerial bombardment of British towns and cities imminent, it seemed inevitable that the whole nation would eventually have to subsist on a siege diet.

In 1940 a committee of food experts was formed to decide on the minimum diet per person upon which the nation could survive and remain in good health. In due time the committee declared that if real siege conditions came to exist in Britain, then the diet of each adult should be a daily ration as follows: twelve ounces of bread, one pound of potatoes, two ounces of oatmeal, one ounce of fat, six ounces of green or root vegetables, and six tenths of a pint of milk. This would have to be supplemented by small but unspecified amounts of meat, fish, cheese, eggs, sugar, and dried or fresh fruits.

In March, 1941, however, President Roosevelt's Lend-Lease Act was passed, and so the grim specter of near-famine hovering over Britain was dispelled. More than this, the act, which brought fresh hope to Britain, struck a telling blow at Nazi Germany, for it provided Britain with United States ships of war and great quantities of arms, munitions, and war materials, besides shiploads of American food, such as dried eggs and milk, canned meats, beans, milk and bacon, cheese and fat. So heartening was this American gesture that many Britons declared they would be happy for Britain to fight the war without the help of the United States Armed Forces, providing the nation continued to receive lend-lease aid.

In the meantime, food rationing was extended to include canned meats, canned fish, and canned vegetables. Fish was already scarce since most of the British fishing trawlers had been requisitioned by the Royal Navy for minesweeping and patrol duties. Because of this, whale, and even shark, meat appeared in British fishmongers' shops for the first time.

In February of 1942, canned fruit, canned tomatoes, and canned peas were rationed; in April, all breakfast cereals and canned milk; in July, syrup and molasses. Soap was rationed to one pound per person per month; and candy and chocolate, to 8 to 12 ounces per person per month.

By 1943 gasoline rationing was so drastic that civilians were allowed no gasoline at all other than the "supplementary rations" allocated to those who could prove beyond all doubt that they needed cars for legitimate business. To be sure, gasoline could be bought on the black market by those with sufficient money and lack of scruples, but heaven help the motorist who was caught with just so much as a gallon of gasoline he could not honestly account for. The fines for this were rightly most severe, and the cost of illegal motoring in Britain during the war could be very high indeed.

To offset the gasoline shortage, British natural gas companies evolved a form of gas propulsion for automobiles, but it never proved popular. The slow and lumbering gas-propelled motor car, with its blisterlike fabric container on the roof was too ludicrous a sight for most self-respecting motorists. Even people who possessed bicycles were lucky, for cycle manufacture had been cut to one-third of peacetime production, and the wartime "utility" model bicycles were unattractive anyway. Farmers and countryfolk who had horses fared better than less fortunate town dwellers, and horseback riders and horse-drawn vehicles once more became familiar sights in the British countryside.

At the outbreak of the war, some 50,000 to 60,000 able-bodied young coal miners, who had already learned more than enough of the futility, dangers, and discomforts of Britain's "Cinderella industry," had joyfully left the coal mines to join the armed forces. British coal mines were thus left with only miners too old to join the forces and those whose health had suffered in the mines and were unfit anyway.

Britain was now desperately short of young, strong men to hew coal; and although the government appealed for 50,000 young and expert miners to return to the mines, the appeal naturally failed. Even the boredom and dangers of service life were infinitely preferable to the reeking damp, the discomfort, and the lethal dust of the deep black "pits."

Thus coal production, fuel, and by-products made from coal fell; and Hugh Dalton, then minister of fuel and power, was forced to initiate fuel rationing. The rations, based on the number of rooms in each house or building, could be taken as coal, gas, electricity, or a combination of all three. The British public were exhorted to save fuel and economize on heating: to switch off all electrical appliances and lights when not in use; to use only one bar of multi-barred electric fires; and to limit the depth of their hot bath water to five inches.

Coal in wartime Britain was truly "black diamonds", and among petty crimes, coal pilfering from coal yards and outside coal bins was common. This led to such extraordinary measures as citizens sitting guard over their coal bins at night and even to booby-trapping coal by inserting small charges of gunpowder into lumps as a somewhat drastic deterrent to coal pilferers.

Clothes rationing was inevitable and drastic. The basic clothes ration for a man worked out at three pairs of sox per year, one shirt every 20 months, one pair of underpants and one undershirt every two years, one vest every five years, one two-piece suit of trousers and jacket every two years, and one overcoat every seven years.

The cost of wartime clothing was prohibitive. A man's made-to-measure suit, which had cost £14 in peacetime, now cost £50. A woman's two-piece costume, which had cost £12, rose to something like £40. A woman's night-dress, which cost £1 10s. in peacetime, now cost £14. With the price of women's hats soaring, women began to evolve their own hat styles, frequently using colored scarves or lengths of brightly colored cloth to make turbans. Because the steel used for their supports was needed for war materials, women's corsets were no longer made.

Silk stockings were as rare as a treasure trove; so in summer the majority of women went bare-legged except on special occasions, and in winter they wore short sox and trousers, an innovation that has proved its practicality. Women's shoe styles became less glamorous, with square toes and flat heels, the high-heeled styles almost vanishing from the shops. Cosmetics too were hard to obtain, and enterprising manufacturers sold "do-it-yourself" cosmetic kits, which women could mix for themselves.

Black marketeers were offering £5 for every book of clothing ration coupons they could lay their grubby fingers on. Secondhand clothes markets also flourished; and the traditional British jumble sale, a peacetime means of raising funds for the church or for charitable purposes, now became one of life's most important events. When a jumble sale was to take place, people queued up for hours beforehand, as they had done for the fall and summer sales of the big stores in peacetime.

In their kitchens the women had to make do with old and worn-out equipment or improvise with items never designed for the purpose since a variety of saucepans, frying pans, kettles, and buckets were no longer available, the metal being diverted into the making of war equipment. The production of domestic chinaware, plates, dishes, cups, and saucers was strictly limited; and such articles were made only in plain white china. Artistic chinaware and ceramics with colored designs were no longer manufactured.

While the women of Britain suffered shortages of the things that were dear and necessary to them, the men of Britain also experienced privations. Beer and tobacco were not rationed but they became increasingly hard to get, increasingly poor in quality, and increasingly expensive. Beer, now often made with oats and potatoes instead of barley, was lower in alcoholic content and specific gravity and poorer in flavor. The whiskey distillers of Scotland manufactured for export only, and to walk into a pub in wartime Britain and ask for whiskey was almost like walking into the Tower of London and asking for the Crown jewels. When this happened, a deathly hush would fall on the people in the pub or tavern or inn as they waited for the reaction of the landlord, who not infrequently exploded into righteous anger. The attitudes of the publicans of Britain was quite understandable in such cases, for so short was the supply of beer and liquor that many taverns, inns, and pubs were very often closed when in peacetime they would have been doing a roaring business. In addition to their beer, tobacco, and liquor, the men went notably short of razor blades; steel was also needed for other and more important purposes. Thus beards came into fashion as they had done in Victorian times.

Supplies of timber for the manufacture of household furniture were drastically reduced, and the small amount of furniture produced was shoddy in construction and poor in design and at first available only to those whose homes were destroyed during the bombing raids. By 1942 the government had reduced the manufacture of domestic furniture to a mere twenty-two items, which were constructed of specified amounts of timber. Plywood was replaced by hardboard, and polished surfaces vanished from the scene altogether.

This furniture was rationed to families whose homes had been destroyed, to newlyweds who were setting up homes, and to couples who were expecting babies. This utility furniture, as it was called, was obtained by means of ration "units," which could also be used for purchasing sheets, blankets, pillow slips, mattresses, linoleum floor covering, carpets, curtains, and towels.

Young couples who were expecting babies were in a difficult plight. Baby carriages were almost nonexistent, and such as were to be had were roughly painted, boxlike monstrosities of cheap plywood, mounted on four small wheels with little rubber blocks instead of the gracefully curved springs of prewar times. Babies' diapers, feeding bottles and rubber nipples, baby baths, baby chamber pots, and all-important metal fireguards to prevent toddlers from falling into open hearths were also hard to otbain.

Children born in those gray and hazardous times entered a world that was almost without toys. The toys being manufactured were ugly to look at, shoddy in construction, sometimes painted with dangerous paints or made of inflammable materials, and extremely expensive. The only toys of that period that were worthy of the name were made by men in the armed services during their off-duty hours far from home and family. These toys were often beautifully made and included colored model airplanes, ships, tanks, rocking horses, wooden dolls, Noah's arks complete with animals, go-carts, dolls' baby carriages, and dolls' houses. Some of these toys, in fact, were such works of creative art that they deserved a place in Britain's Imperial War Museum as the testimony of the love of Britain's fighting men for the children from whom they were parted.

Even if deprived of baby carriages, diapers, and store-bought toys, the wartime babies and children of Britain were well cared for in other ways. They received regular and ample supplies of high-grade orange juice, vitamins, cod-liver oil, and National Dried Milk. In fact, great numbers of Britain's wartime babies developed into far finer physical specimens than their parents, who had not been so well cherished during World War I.

In the meantime, while the British public was in the grip of an era of ever-growing austerity and scarcity, the government was in the grip of ever-growing turmoil.

3. Winston Churchill Becomes Prime Minister

PRIME MINISTER NEVILLE CHAMBERLAIN fell from power because of his government's ineffectual handling of Britain's war effort, including war industry, aggravated by the distrust and hostility that existed between the Conservative Government and the powerful Socialist trade unions. Chamberlain's downfall was also accelerated by the failure of the Scandinavian campaign.

On April 8–9, 1940, Germany had invaded Norway. One reason for the invasion was to ensure the continuation of the ten million tons of iron ore that were shipped annually to Germany from the ice-free port of Narvik. The other reason was that Hitler's naval Chiefs of Staff, Grand Admiral Raeder and Admiral Doenitz, needed Norwegian ports as bases for submarines and commerce raiders.

On April 12, 1940, a British amphibious expedition left for Narvik Fjord to counter the German invasion. Admiral Lord Cork was in command of the naval forces and General Mackesy in command of the military. Admiral Lord Cork was dashing and intrepid whereas General Mac-

kesy was overcautious; and as there was no supreme commander to coordinate the operation, it was a failure.

Eventually, 24,000 British, French, and Polish troops,
together with their stores and equipment, had to be re-
embarked from Norway to help meet the mounting German pressure on the western front. The German invasion
of Norway and Denmark was complete. To quote Winston Churchill, "Britain has been forestalled, surprised and
outwitted in spite of our overwhelmingly superior naval
strength."

A wave of anger and frustration swept the whole of
Britain; and when the Government and the Opposition
met in the House of Commons on May 7, 1940 to debate
the failure of the campaign, the atmosphere was hostile
and bitter.

Prime Minister Chamberlain opened the debate by
stating to the assembly that the withdrawal of the last of
the British forces from Trondheim was complete. Clement
Attlee, Socialist member and later to be prime minister,
bitterly reminded the grim-faced members of the assembly
that everywhere the story was the same "too late!"

Admiral of the Fleet Sir Roger Keys, dressed in his full
uniform, presumably to give weight to words that needed
no stressing, opened his speech by saying, "I wish to speak
for some officers and men of the fighting, seagoing navy who
are very unhappy . . ." Sir Roger Keys was not a good
speaker; but when he had finished, he had revealed to the
assembly a deadly weakness in Britain's war effort: no
fixity of purpose and no coordination within the fighting
services. The admiral's speech carried enormous weight,
for he was known to be a fighting man with no political
ambitions.

Mr. David Lloyd George, Mr. Duff Cooper, and Mr. Stafford Cripps also strongly attacked the prime minister's handling of the war, but the most bitter attack of all came from an unexpected quarter—his old friend, colleague, and onetime admirer, Mr. Leo Amery. Like nails into Chamberlain's political coffin, Amery hammered home the weaknesses and failures of the Chamberlain Government, quoting in his ferocious attack Oliver Cromwell when he dissolved the British government known in history as the Long Parliament: "You have sat here too long for any good you have been doing. Depart, I say, and let us have done with you. In the name of God, go!" It has since been accepted that Leo Amery's speech destroyed the Chamberlain Government.

There was now a crisis within the government at what was probably the most perilous time in the history of Britain, and a vote was taken in the House of Commons to determine whether the Chamberlain Government should remain in office. There were 281 in favor of the government's remaining and 200 against. Although the government had a majority of 81 votes, this was considered insufficient because when the voting figures were analyzed, it was established that 43 Conservatives had voted against the government while an additional 80 members had abstained or been absent.

On the day after the Norway debate, a resolution was passed by a large majority of members that a new government should be formed that should consist of members of all three parties, Conservative, Labour, and Liberal. Leo Amery and some 60 Conservative members who had voted against the government or who had abstained, informed Neville Chamberlain that they would not join or support any government that did not fulfill these conditions, but that they would support any leader, including Chamberlain, who could form such a coalition. The Labour party, on the other hand, declared unanimously that they would serve in a coalition government under any leader *except* Chamberlain.

It was now obvious that Neville Chamberlain could not remain as prime minister, and on May 9, 1940, four men met in the Cabinet Room of the House of Commons to decide who should be his successor. They were Neville Chamberlain, Lord Halifax, Winston Churchill, and David Margesson, the Conservative chief whip (an official appointed to keep discipline and secure the attendance of, and give necessary information to, members of his party in the House of Commons).

Neville Chamberlain declared that he would be prepared to serve either Lord Halifax or Churchill. Churchill, on the other hand, refused to serve under Lord Halifax, who, in any case, declared that his peerage would prevent him from entering the House of Commons as prime minister. In this manner, Winston Churchill emerged as Britain's prime minister and war leader.

So it was that on May 10, 1940, the same day on which the Nazi tanks and troops poured triumphantly into Holland and Belgium, Neville Chamberlain tendered his resignation as prime minister to King George VI. Winston Churchill, then first lord of the Admiralty, was summoned to Buckingham Palace and asked to form a coalition government composed of members of all three political parties. This he agreed to do.

On May 13, 1940, speaking as prime minister, Winston Churchill addressed the House of Commons:

You ask what is our policy? I will say that it is to wage war by sea, land and air with all our might and all the strength that God can give us; to wage war against a monstrous tyranny never surpassed in the dark lamentable catalogue of human crime. That is our policy. You ask what is our aim? I can answer in one word—*Victory*. Victory at all costs, victory in spite of all terror, victory however long and hard the road may be, for without victory there is no survival.

These were not the words of a politician; rather were they the words of a medieval warlord to his warriors. And it was a mighty warlord indeed that Britain needed now.

The members of the House of Commons rose to him as one man, for Winston's words put fresh heart into them and roused the ancient spirit of the British people, who are the deadliest fighters when facing the most desperate odds.

It is hard to believe that these fiery and immortal words were uttered by a man who had once fumbled to a halt during his speech to the House of Commons many years before and sat down in embarrassed silence. As unbelievable as it may seem, Winston Churchill was no natural orator, for he had never even been to a British university or joined a debating society. He learned his oratory the hard way, in the harsh rough-and-tumble of party politics. And never was this hard-learned oratory to stand a hard-pressed nation in such good stead.

Hitler's Germany must have rejoiced when it learned that Winston Churchill was now Britain's prime minister and war leader. In 1942, when Britain's fortunes were at low ebb, Dr. Goebbels, Hitler's chief of propaganda, wrote in his diary, "The Führer recalls that all Englishmen whom he received before the outbreak of war were in agreement that Churchill was a fool. Even Chamberlain said so to the Führer."

Both Hitler and his English informants were very badly misled, for Winston Churchill, far from being a fool, was a political maverick, whose loyalty was to his country and not to any political party. Between the years 1900 and 1964, Churchill unashamedly offered his political allegiance to the Conservatives, the Liberals, the National Liberals, the Constitutionalists, and finally to the Conservatives once more. He was by British political standards an "outsider"; but unlike the vast majority of politicians, Winston had a strong taste for the stimulus of physical danger.

By political "string pulling" when he was only twenty-four, Winston Churchill, a civilian, charged with the British lancers against the dervish army at the Battle of Omdurman. He deliberately put himself in a position of mortal danger just for the sheer exhilaration of it and the drug-soaked dervishes could take all six shots from a .38 revolver through the body and still have strength enough to decapitate an enemy with their fearful two-handed swords. Afterwards, Winston Churchill coolly remarked of this experience, "There is nothing more exhilarating than to be shot at without result."

A year after the Omdurman episode, Churchill, now war correspondent with the *Morning Post* during the Boer War, was captured by the Boers when he was riding on an armored train, and sent to a prisoner-of-war camp at Pretoria. He escaped from this camp by calmly jumping over a wall and walking through the town, and he eventually arrived at Durban, Natal, with a reward of £25 on his head, "dead or alive."

It was most probably this love of living dangerously that earned Winston Churchill the reputation of being a fool from people who did not know better. Churchill was a unique combination of a fighting man first and a states-man second, a potent factor in the downfall of the Axis powers.

As the grandson of the mighty duke of Marlborough, it was natural that he should be a blue-blooded fighting aristocrat. The trouble was that he did not conform to con-vention, which was, and still is, a grave social sin among Britain's ruling classes.

For example, he approved the abdication of the popu-lar Edward, Prince of Wales, who became King Edward VIII for less than a year. For supporting this abdication, Churchill incurred the bitter hostility of the House of Commons, and it almost smashed his political career.

In his youthful days in politics, Churchill had been called "the most hated man in the House of Commons" and "a traitor to his class." In these days he was openly snubbed by the wealthy, class-conscious Conservatives, who banned him from their sumptuous country houses.

Churchill was also the man who dispensed with polite and formal platitudes, calling Hitler "a bloodthirsty gutter-snipe" and the wolfish Stalin "Uncle Joe." He was no re-specter of persons and admired this characteristic in other people.

He needed all his wide experience, courage, and élan to deal with his terrible and overwhelming task now, for there were many political enemies to be reconciled before the coalition government could possibly succeed.

Winston Churchill's first weeks as prime minister were very difficult for him. When he rose to address the assembly in the House of Commons, the Conservatives remained silent and hostile. It was a dangerous situation, not only for Churchill but for the whole of Britain, for diplomats and newspapermen from other countries were beginning to say that Churchill did not have the full support of the government he led.

One day, however, when Churchill rose to make a speech, David Margesson, the Conservative chief whip, suddenly stood up and beckoned the hitherto silent Conservatives to their feet. They responded and began to cheer Churchill, who was so overcome that he wept openly. It is believed that Neville Chamberlain brought about this reconciliation after he had been told by Paul Einzig, a journalist who worked in the House of Commons, of the ominous things foreign representatives and newsmen were saying.

Neville Chamberlain was no war leader, but his generosity of spirit to his rival in the hour of Britain's desperate crisis marked his greatness as a man and as a statesman. It was however, a magnanimity that some of Chamberlain's closest friends did not share, and they maintained a smoldering resentment against Churchill for the remainder of their lives.

Although the majority of the Conservative party accepted Churchill, he had yet to win the confidence of the Socialists. A lesser man would have failed utterly in this delicate and, in view of the country's plight, dangerous undertaking. One false step, and he would have thrown the nation into political conflict that could well have lost the war before it had hardly begun.

In the past Churchill had done a great deal to earn the dislike and distrust of the Socialists, for he had deliberately broken with the Liberal party because it had supported the Socialists led by Ramsay MacDonald. They also remembered how, in 1922, after being kicked out of the Radical party of Dundee, which he had served for 14 years, he boldly gave his allegiance to the Conservative party in 1924, when he became Conservative member for Epping in the county of Essex. Moreover, he had added insult to injury by saying, when upbraided for his political turnabout, "Anyone can rat, but it takes a certain amount of ingenuity to re-rat."

It was this same disregard for conventional political principles and the vast experience he had gained in the political bearpits of Britain, together with his granite will, dynamic driving power, courage, and contempt for physical danger that made Winston Churchill the leader Britain so desperately needed now.

And there was no time to lose.

Swiftly setting about the task of forming Britain's wartime national government, Churchill made Socialist Mr. Clement Attlee lord privy seal and also his deputy in the House of Commons. Socialist Arthur Greenwood became minister without portfolio, that is, a Cabinet minister who is not in charge of any government department.

It was a shrewd and tactful move by Churchill to appease the suspicious Socialists, for it gave two of their members two of the six seats on the War Cabinet, the inner circle of ministers who controlled the government. The other four members of the Cabinet were Conservatives: Churchill himself, Lord Halifax, Anthony Eden, and Neville Chamberlain, who retired from office on October 3, 1940, and died on November 9 of the same year.

Socialist member Ernest Morrison, whose name later

became synonymous with Morrison indoor air raid shelters, was minister of supply; Socialist member Hugh Dalton, minister of economic warfare; Conservative member A. V. Alexander took Churchill's old post as first lord of the Admiralty. Socialist member Sir Stafford Cripps became Russian ambassador; and Lord Beaverbrook, the Canadian who had been financier, Unionist member of Parliament, and newspaper tycoon, was minister of aircraft.

Burly and forthright Socialist Ernest Bevin, leader of Britain's largest and most powerful trade union, the Transport and General Workers' Union, became minister of labour. Fiery-tempered Socialist Emanuel Shinwell was offered a post as undersecretary, which he scornfully rejected. "Manny," as his friends and associates called him, remembered how Churchill had slighted the Socialists in the past.

Churchill did not treat the Liberal party as generously as he did the Socialists in forming his government. The Liberal leader, Sir Archibald Sinclair, was made air minister, but with no place in the War Cabinet. Sir John Anderson, whose name, like Ernest Morrison's, was to become associated with air raid shelters, was home secretary. Sir Kingsley Wood was chancellor of the exchequer, Lord Cranbourne was paymaster general, and Mr. Duff Cooper was head of the Ministry of Information.

Such was the national government of Britain at the beginning of World War II, and never was there one less representative of British peacetime politics. But it was the only form of government that could hope to lead the nation in the awful conflict soon to come.

In the meantime, Winston Churchill had added the office of minister of defense to his office of prime minister, at a stroke assuming powers both civil and military and thus making himself infinitely more powerful than any peacetime prime minister. In doing this, he also made himself indispensable to Britain, a fact freely admitted by the national daily *The Times* in the dark days of September, 1941. Winston Churchill was now 65 years old, 15 years older than his arch enemy, Adolf Hitler, and if he had been an ordinary working man, he would have been retired and living on the old-age pension.

Throughout history, great leaders of men and nations have frequently been noted for an ability to see into the future, and Winston Churchill did not lack this quality. Right from the very beginning, he knew that America would throw her mighty weight in with Britain against the Nazis. At the very beginning of the war, he told Paul Reynaud, premier of France, that together Britain and America would starve Germany out, burn her crops and forests, and burn and destroy her towns. But it was doubtful if even he could see then the awful retribution that British and American bombers would at last wreak on the Third Reich.

The "nerve center" of Britain's war command was established 35 feet below ground under the Ministry of Defense Building at Storey's Gate, London. It was a maze of offices and corridors of massively reinforced concrete and steel girders, where 300 men who planned and directed Britain's war effort ate and slept and rarely saw the light of day above ground.

Here was Churchill's lair, a place called the Annex, an austere and almost comfortless little chamber with a small desk, on which stood two candles and a large electric flashlight for use should enemy bombers destroy and disrupt London's power supplies. Beyond the desk was the single bed in which he slept.

Next door to the Annex was the Map Room, guarded

night and day by a Royal Marine sentry, armed with rifle and bayonet. In this room, with its red, green, and white "scrambler" telephones, information from all battlefronts was collected at regular four-hour intervals. This was the grim place of which Winston Churchill said, "If the invasion comes, that's where I'll sit. I'll sit there until the Germans are driven back or they carry me out—dead!"

But it was not Winston Churchill who died in his concrete lair beneath London. It was Adolf Hitler who died by his own hand in a concrete bunker beneath Berlin.

4. Britain Prepares for Invasion

AT THE OUTBREAK of the war, a British Expeditionary Force of over 300,000 men had been sent to aid France, Belgium, and Holland against the Nazis. The BEF was a large army, but woefully weak in firepower. Three divisions were without artillery, and the only armor consisted of two tank battalions of 100 puny four- to five-ton tanks. In addition to this weakness, the Allies were totally unprepared for the smashing blows of the swiftly moving heavy tanks and armored fighting vehicles of the German panzer divisions in a totally new type of war called *Blitzkreig* or "lightning war."

In May, 1940, the French army and the British Expeditionary Forces, moving into the Low Countries to counter the enemy advance, were overwhelmed by the speed, firepower, and ferocity of the German armored divisions.

On May 14, 1940, the city of Rotterdam was bombed by the Luftwaffe, and on May 15 the Dutch army surrendered to the Nazis. That same day, sweeping forward like a cyclone of fire and steel, the German armored divisions crossed the River Meuse and took the British and French armies in the rear. Paul Reynaud, the French premier, immediately telephoned Winston Churchill and told him that France was a defeated nation. On May 16, at Sedan, the French army disintegrated under the German attack.

Regardless of personal danger, Winston Churchill rushed to Paris with his staff for an emergency conference with Paul Reynaud and General Gamelin, who with a large map explained the military plight of France. Pointing at a bulge marked in red on the map, General Gamelin told Churchill that this was the spot where the fate of France and Britain was at stake. Churchill then told Paul Reynaud that even if France was overwhelmed and beaten by the Nazis, Britain would go on fighting alone until the United States came to her aid.

In the meantime, the armored might of Germany swept relentlessly and resistlessly through Belgium and occupied the city of Brussels. At this moment, the entire British nation was nearer to panic than at any time in its long and turbulent history. The whole nation thought that it could only be a matter of days, perhaps merely hours, before the German hordes swarmed across the twenty-one miles of the English Channel to invade Britain. So black was the prospect that the United States Embassy advised all its nationals in Britain at the time to return home as fast as they could.

Many Americans ignored this warning; some stayed to join the British Armed Forces and others to form an American squadron of the Local Defense Volunteers to protect London against invasion. Most people at that time thought it would come in the form of a massive attack by paratroopers dropped from fleets of German aircraft.

In the meantime, the German tanks and infantry swept triumphantly towards the Channel coast of France, leaving the best part of the British Expeditionary Force and thousands of French and Belgian soldiers surrounded and cut off not far from Dunkirk. These, the Nazis decided, could be dealt with later.

This was the first massive error on the part of the German High Command; for instead of annihilating the more than 300,000 British soldiers and the thousands of French and Belgian allies, the German armor clanked to a halt. The Germans believed that their powerful Luftwaffe would prevent Lord Gort, who commanded the BEF, from evacuating the beaten British army from Dunkirk.

Although the aircraft of the Luftwaffe did bomb and machine-gun the exhausted and wounded British and Allied soldiers who streamed in tens of thousands across the Dunkirk beaches to the fleet of rescuing ships and boats, they did not prevent the evacuation.

This evacuation of an entire army was a unique combined operation by ships of the Royal Navy, Merchant Navy, Southern Railway's cross-Channel ferryboats, paddle steamers used as peacetime pleasure craft, lifeboats of the Royal National Lifeboat Institution, and tugboats. An appeal broadcast by the BBC added hundreds of private yachts, fishing boats, shrimpers, small motorboats, and even sailing dinghies to the rescue fleet.

R.A.F. air cover of the evacuation was only partial. A number of rescue vessels were bombed and sunk, and many rescuers and rescued were killed or wounded. Because of this, there was much bitter criticism of the R.A.F. by the survivors. They could not know at that terrible moment that the few precious combat aircraft of the Royal Air Force were being kept to smash the air fleets of the Luftwaffe spearheading the Nazi invasion of Britain, which now seemed imminent.

And the individual tragedies and dramas of the evacuation were not confined to the ravaged beaches of Dunkirk.

One early morning before dawn, the crew of the North Goodwin lightship, which marks the northern extremity of the deadly, ten-mile Goodwin Sands, heard a shout in the darkness. "Lightship, ahoy. Can we come alongside?"

"Lay off until daylight, when we can see you," the lightshipmen shouted back. It was wise not to take chances at this period.

At daybreak a gray-painted gunboat of the Royal Navy came alongside the lightship and tied up. The gunboat was crammed with French marines, filthy, emaciated. Some were wounded, and some were dying. Some muttered and moaned to themselves.

They had spent 12 days without food or water on a half-sunk wrecked ship off the French coast, in mortal terror of being seen by enemy surface craft or aircraft. A young French officer, little more than a boy, wept as he told how he had had to shoot three of his own men who had gone raving mad and tried to bayonet their own comrades. The crew of the gunboat and the crew of the lightship did what they could to ease and comfort these pitiful wrecks of war, and then the gunboat took them ashore to be landed at Ramsgate, a peacetime holiday resort on the coast of Kent.

Ten miles to the south, at the other extremity of the Goodwin Sands, a small, wooden fishing trawler with a Boulogne registration number, ripped and splintered with machine gun bullets and cannon shells, drifted helplessly alongside the South Goodwin lightship.

When the lightship crew had made the trawler fast, they just stood and gazed with shock and horror at what they saw. The little wooden fishing boat, slowly sinking, was packed with English and French soldiers, all wounded, some dying, some dead. In its bilges, water, blood, red wine from shattered bottles, and long French loaves, swilled back and forth; an unholy sacrament to Mars, the god of war.

In the shell-splintered ruin of the small wheelhouse at the foot of the shattered steering wheel lay a man without a leg and without a head. One of the survivors told the lightship crew that he had been steering the trawler towards England when a swathe of 20 mm cannon shells from a marauding Messerschmitt 109 Nazi combat plane had ripped into the trawler like a band saw, killing and wounding many of the escapees and blowing the leg off the man at the wheel. He propped himself up and continued to steer until a second blast from the merciless Messerschmitt decapitated him. After that, the trawler had just drifted until it came to the lightship.

The lightship master called up the Coastguards, and shortly afterwards a fast rescue launch came out to take the survivors and the dead from the trawler, which was then left to sink.

These were but two of innumerable terrible incidents that happened during "the miracle of Dunkirk."

On June 27, 1940, 8,000 men were brought safely home from those bomb-, shell-, and bullet-blasted beaches of Dunkirk; 18,000 were rescued on June 28; 47,000, on June 31; and 64,000, on July 1.

The total number of men rescued from Dunkirk was

338,260 (225,000 of these were British), and they were succored by the strangest, most gallant fleet of ships ever to sail the seas.

The whole of Britain's southern and southeastern coast was in a turmoil as the rescued soldiers poured ashore. What was most noticeable was that they did not have the looks of defeated men. They were all filthy dirty, all exhausted, some walking, some limping, many being carried on stretchers; but one and all they were angry and defiant.

"We'll be back," some of them shouted, shaking their grimy fists towards the smoking coast of France. "We'll be back, you German bastards!" they bellowed, maddened with anger and frustration at the thought of the guns, vehicles, and ammunition dumps they had been forced to abandon.

The great holiday resorts of the coasts of south and southeast England were used to dealing with tens of thousands of holidaymakers in peacetime, but never had they dealt with such an overwhelming torrent as now. The rescued soldiers poured into pubs and taverns, which they soon drank dry; and as they drank, they bitterly condemned those who they said had allowed this thing to happen.

The entire British nation rejoiced at the miraculous delivery of the men of the British Expeditionary Force, but Winston Churchill soon ruthlessly destroyed this mood of dangerous euphoria. In the House of Commons he told the tense listeners that Dunkirk, far from being something to rejoice at, was a terrible military disaster and that the invasion of Britain could well be imminent.

It was at this black moment in British history that Winston Churchill made one of his famous fighting speeches, which did so much to strengthen the spirit and the will of the British people. "We shall go on to the end," he said. "We shall fight in France. We shall fight on the seas and on the oceans. We shall fight with ever-growing strength in the air; we shall defend our island whatever the cost may be. We shall fight on the beaches; we shall fight on the landing grounds; we shall fight in the fields and in the streets; we shall fight in the hills. We will never surrender." And this was not just rhetoric, for Winston Churchill knew the British people.

The tens of thousands who had guns were prepared to use them, eager to use them, even though they knew the terrible odds against survival. Those who had no arms sought where they might find them.

Meanwhile, the all-victorious Nazis made what is now known to be one of their mistakes that helped to lose them the war. Instead of following up their victory at Dunkirk and pursuing to its home shores a defeated, disorganized, and almost weaponless army, the Germans struck southwards into France and thus gave Britain breathing space.

The French soldiers who had escaped to Britain gallantly returned to France to continue the temporarily hopeless fight for their country. They went in two hastily formed divisions to help the lone 51st Highland Division of Scotland, which was fighting with true, inspired Gaelic ferocity. That ferocity had earned the kilted Scotsmen the title, in World War I, of "the Women of Hell" from the admiring Germans. Some 8,000 of these gallant Highlanders were taken prisoner, although about 136,000 Scots and Allied troops eventually escaped back to Britain in another series of small evacuations.

For the moment Britain stood alone against the Nazis. Yet Winston Churchill could predict: "For a thousand years men will say—this was their finest hour."

Once the immediate shock of threatened invasion had

worn off and the invasion did not come, the naturally phleg-
matic character of the British people reasserted itself. In
spite of the awful danger that threatened, the British public continued its way of life much as it had done in peacetime.

People still went to football and cricket matches at
weekends; to cinemas, theaters, and dance halls. They went
walking round the heavily sandbagged streets and through
the parks. Moreover, those who could get gasoline by one
means or another still went for automobile drives around
those parts of the country that were not restricted "war
zones." The British Broadcasting Corporation still broadcast sports items, including football matches and horse
racing.

Many of the younger people began to find the threat
of invasion was stimulating and exciting. And what was
astonishing, especially to foreigners, the British public
loudly aired its grievances on trivial matters, seeming to ig-
nore the threat of invasion entirely.

During the week men growled and swore and blamed
the government for everything, including the chaos and inconvenience caused by the blackout. At weekends the
same men grunted, puffed and panted, and blamed the
government for everything as they dug deep holes in their
gardens in which to erect the cramped, steel Anderson
air raid shelters. Later they and their families were to spend
much of their waking time and all of their sleeping time in
these shelters, which were eventually used by about half the
population of Britain.

In the meantime, the workers grumbled about the increase of the standard rate of income tax to 8s. 6d. in the £1,
and the rich complained bitterly about surtax. Rich and

poor, to say nothing of the Socialist members of the coalition government, complained about the newly introduced purchase tax on goods.

The whole nation was loud in its protests about the increasing prices and the scarcity of beer, liquor, and tobacco, but this was as nothing compared to the hurricane blast of national disapproval at the rationing of that sacred British prerogative—*tea*.

In the early stages of the war, in spite of food rationing and general scarcity, it did not seem to occur to the British that their country was under siege. When Benito Mussolini had thrown in the Italians with the Nazis on June 10, 1940, he had closed the Mediterranean Sea to Allied shipping. Ships carrying war materials and food now had to make the long and perilous passage round the Cape of Good Hope to get to Britain. These conditions made it essential to restrict drastically all consumer goods for the home market and direct the workers and the raw materials used for making them into the war factories.

So it was that the Limitation of Supplies Order was passed by the Government; under this order the production of all goods not essential to the war effort was stopped.

It became the gigantic task of the newly appointed minister of labour, Ernest Bevin, to see that this order was speedily implemented, and to this end the trade unions of Britain pledged Bevin their unanimous support.

This capable, onetime trade union leader, now a very powerful minister indeed, was swift to act. After he had met with the British Employers Federation and the Trades Union Congress (TUC), Order 1305 emerged. From that moment, strikes on the part of the workers and lockouts on the part of employers became illegal. Bevin did not intend to see Britain's war machine sabotaged by industrial disputes.

Before the ruthless urging of dynamic Lord Beaverbrook and the dogged determination of Ernest Morrison, British war factories began to hum, with workers doing shift-work for 24 hours a day and seven days a week and the traditional British Whitsun and August national holidays indefinitely suspended.

Both men and women toiled like galley slaves and a 70-hour working week became commonplace. When it was seen that the unremitting toil was affecting the workers' health and thus having an adverse effect on production, Ernest Bevin wisely limited the working hours of women factory workers to 60 a week and suggested the same hours for men.

Lord Beaverbrook would not agree to this, and so the workers in the aircraft factories he controlled continued to slog out a seven-day week, making the aircraft that would soon save Britain not only from invasion but from annihilation also.

Other British men and women were working their hearts out at this desperate period too. They were engaged on the vital defense system that was to give British combat plane pilots the mastery over the Luftwaffe in the Battle of Britain so soon to come. That system was *radar*.

And while the men and women in Britain's war factories were toiling at ever increasing tempo, the threat of invasion hung over the land. Everywhere preparations for the defense of the island were becoming more evident.

Fields and downlands, parks and parklands, golf courses and playing fields were littered and barricaded with anything that would wreck or impede landing aircraft. Everything imaginable was used—old automobiles, old iron boilers, old stoves, iron baths, kitchen sinks, massive chunks of scrap metal, farm carts and tractors, and hundreds of thousands of old motor and tractor tires. Iron scaffolding and girders were erected to form massive barricades to impale aircraft and vehicles, a form of defense known as *chevaux-de-frise*, once used to break up charging cavalry.

Fifteen-hundred-pound blocks of cement were placed in position, where they could be drawn across roads. All nameplates were removed from signposts, road direction systems, and railway stations in order to confuse the enemy when he came. Concrete blockhouses were built at crossroads and other strategic points. Huge, pyramid-shaped, concrete "dragon's teeth," devised to rip the tracks from tanks and armored half-track vehicles, sprang up across plowed fields and any open spaces.

The lonely and deserted beaches of sourthern and eastern England were a maze of barbed wire, land mines in the tens of thousands, and steel chevaux-de-frise to impale landing assault craft. Concealed oil pipes thrust out beneath the sea to pump out oil and swiftly envelop enemy invasion craft in a sea of flame. Huge cannon, ranging from six to sixteen-inch caliber, covered the 21-mile-wide Strait of Dover, whence it was thought the invaders would come.

Careful measures were taken to make sure that motor vehicles and gasoline and diesel fuel would not fall into the invaders' hands. Private owners of automobiles were ordered to immobilize their vehicles at night under a penalty of £50. The wheels of public coaches and buses were locked when left unattended. Gasoline service stations on the invasion coasts were drastically reduced in number, and those remaining were guarded by armed sentries with instructions to destroy the stations rather than let them fall into the hands of the enemy. Armored trains guarded railway stations, marshalling yards, freight depots, and the rolling stock of Britain's railways.

By September, 1940, Britain had 27 divisions to defend the home front. These divisions, however had received very little training, and service rifles were in such short supply that drills were performed with broomsticks, pick-shafts, pitchforks, and any domestic or agricultural tool or implement available. Official circulars were issued, asking private owners of firearms to deliver their weapons to the police for distribution to the armed forces. Although an amnesty was declared for those who held firearms illegally, only about 20,000 rifles, shotguns, and pistols were collected.

General Ironside, commander in chief, home forces, in an appeal to the public for arms said, "Do not despise your shotguns. We have a million charges of buckshot that would kill a leopard at 200 yards."

King George VI, almost as great a shot as his father, King George V, had been, gave his entire battery of magnificent shotguns to the Home Guard. Retired ex-Indian Army officers gave their ceremonial swords. Collectors of weapons flooded Home Guard posts with spears, ancient swords, and battle-axes, medieval maces and clubs from Africa; daggers of every conceivable shape, age, and origin; and even jungle bush-knives. Britain's archery clubs were training to shoot descending paratroopers, and women carried little packets of pepper to throw into the eyes of the enemy.

It all seemed as ridiculous as brandishing a feather

duster at a rogue elephant about to charge, but at least it showed that the British people were aware of their imminent peril.

In the meantime, thousands of men had responded to Anthony Eden's call to form a civilian defense force called the Local Defence Volunteers, the LDVs for short. Such matters as medical fitness and age were largely ignored. The only requirement was that entrants should be screened as carefully as possible in order to make sure that they were not members of the insidious fifth column. These were the traitors who betrayed their own countries in many instances and who had helped Germany to overthrow France, Belgium, and Holland.

The fact that the German High Command declared that members of the LDV were guerrillas and would be shot out of hand when caught, made no difference. By the summer of 1940, one and a half million men and youths were wearing the armband of the LDV, which at that time was their only uniform. The LDVs were composed of every class and category and included shopkeepers, factory workers, schoolteachers, and tens of thousands of commuters, who worked in the towns and cities, but had their homes in the country.

At the beginning, the LDV, to some degree, was better armed than the regular divisions of the home front, for in the ranks were numbers of retired army officers, gamekeepers, farmers, farmhands, and even professional poachers, who had their own shotguns and rifles.

The overall command of the LDV was the responsibility of General Ironside, and the chief commands were naturally given to retired army officers or to business executives used to handling men. To begin with, men without guns had to share a precious rifle with others and sometimes as many as ten men shared one rifle. The rest had to make do with knives, axes, steel golf clubs, and truncheons, although one LDV group in the county of Lancashire was able to obtain a number of ancient rifles that had seen service in the Crimean War 85 years before.

At this period there was even talk of repelling the enemy with pikes if the worst came to the worst. Nobody cared to consider how the pike-wielders would have got close enough to the enemy to use them.

Large factories, industries, and public services had their own defense organization; and miners, factory workers, and railwaymen coming off night shift would automatically take over guard duties of the places where they worked. Communication networks had to be kept from the enemy at all costs; and the British Broadcasting Corporation, the General Post Office, and the national daily newspapers also organized the defense of their premises and equipment.

At the very beginning, the LDV was little better than a poorly armed mob whose only common denominator was the LDV armband and the iron determination to kill as many Germans as they could before their own turn came to die.

The chaos that existed in the early days of the LDV was not without humor, nevertheless, and the humorous spirit of those far-from-funny times has been captured in a popular British television series called "Dad's Army," which has also been made into a film.

By 1942 the LDV had changed its name to the Home Guard, which consisted of reasonably well-drilled, highly enthusiastic members, now dressed in khaki serge uniforms and steel helmets and all now armed with rifles, many of which had been supplied by the United States. Where the members of the LDV had just been ordinary civilians prepared to defend their country to the last, the Home Guard was rapidly becoming a very formidable guerrilla force indeed.

A private training school, sponsored by wealthy patrons, was opened at Asterly Park in the county of Middlesex. Here, under the expert tuition of a man named Tom Winteringham, who had commanded the British Contingent of the International Brigade during the Spanish civil war, Home Guard personnel were taught the lethal arts of true guerrilla warfare: the destruction of tanks and armored vehicles by sticky bombs and petrol bombs; how to use high explosive for sabotage; how to ambush; the grim business of street-to-street fighting; how to stab sentries silently to death; and how to decapitate them with wire cheese cutters.

This school for slaughter proved so eminently successful that eventually the government took it over, and it became known as War Office No. 1 School. In view of the lethal skills of its teachers and its deadly curriculum, *school* was indeed a most deceptive title.

The task of the ever-increasingly efficient Home Guard was to help defend the southern and southeastern coasts of England, where the enemy invasion forces seemed likely to land. In addition to this, the Home Guard had constantly to guard and, if necessary, defend aircraft production and tank and arms factories. For the protection of such high-priority establishments, small armored cars called Beaverbugs after their sponsor, Lord Beaverbrook, made their appearance.

In addition to these tasks, the Home Guard had to protect and defend airfields and public utilities, keep vigilant watch for enemy saboteurs and fifth columnists, and guard all roadblocks. They had the power to stop and search all vehicles and to check the identity cards that all civilians had to carry.

It was wise to stop when challenged by the Home Guard, for they had very itchy trigger fingers. And who could blame them for shooting at motorists who were reckless enough to drive on when challenged? In those perilous days, the most innocent-looking strangers might be German paratroopers or saboteurs in disguise.

As it transpired, the British Home Guard was never fated to meet Nazi paratroopers in battle, but the Home Guard did capture one Nazi. On May 10, 1941, Rudolf Hess, Hitler's favored protégé, flew a Messerschmitt combat plane solo from Germany to Scotland without Hitler's knowledge. Hess landed near the home of the duke of Hamilton, to whom he hoped to make peace proposals on his own initiative. Members of the 3rd Renfrewshire (Scotland) Battalion of the Home Guard captured him, unaware of the identity of their prisoner. Winston Churchill ordered Hess to be confined in a house near London as a prisoner of war and ordered that no mention of Hess was to be made in the news media. Two days after Hess arrived in Britain, the Nazis' radio broadcasts said that the reason Rudolf Hess had left Germany was that he was an increasingly sick man suffering from obsessions. In any event his one-man peace mission, if that is what it was, came to nothing.

In the meantime, the hidden threat of the deadly fifth column was very real, causing greater concern in Britain than the thought of invasion. Uniformed invaders could be seen and shot at but a fifth columnist might be anybody at all—your milkman, the postman, your neighbor, the man in the store, or even friends and aquaintances you had known for years.

There was no way of identifying a fifth columnist until it was too late; and the threat and uncertainty were made a great deal worse by the thousands of Belgian, Dutch, Polish, French, and Czech refugees now in Britain. In fact, it was taken for granted that the fifth column was already in Britain and only waiting for the invasion to happen. Even Winston Churchill himself admitted this grim fact.

One had to be very, very careful indeed as to what one said and did at this time. Under Defence Regulation 18B, the home secretary had enormous and unprecedented powers. Literally anybody, irrespective of rank or social position, could be arrested and imprisoned without warning.

At this time many warnings and exhortations in poster form were exhibited everywhere in public places. They read: "Careless talk costs lives" and "Join Britain's Silent Column."

The "silent column" was a group formed to counter the fifth column. Its members were told to be discreet, wear no uniforms, and use only common sense, ears, and tongue as weapons. It provided five ways in which to stop careless or defeatist talk, ways that, quite frankly, were methods of intimidation, the most effective one being the ostentatious writing down of the name and words of anyone who might be talking carelessly.

One public exhortation against careless talk backfired badly. It was a poster with the words "Be like Dad. Keep Mum." It was meant to be a clever play on words, for *mum* is British slang for both *mother* and *silent*. It understandably roused the anger of tens of thousands of British *mums,* who were working just as hard as the dads in war factories and earning just as much money and sometimes even more.

A spate of warning notices and posters appeared on the walls of taverns, inns, pubs, public toilets, railway stations, bus depots, and every conceivable place where the public could read them. Many of these posters were silly and childish, and some were downright offensive. Especially offensive were the defeatist characters like Mr. Glumpot, the Defeatist; Mr. Knowall, who knows nothing; and Miss Leakeymouth. These ill-timed and stupid posters not only aroused public anger and contempt, but also created the kind of ill will and mischief that the fifth column thrived on. Because of these posters, quite a number of people informed on others, and many people were arrested for "talking defeat."

So furious was the British public about this that the Ministry of Information had to try other methods. The public was now told to grumble and complain as loudly and about everything as it wished, but to keep silent about the things that mattered.

In the meantime, the security police were very busy indeed. Sir Oswald Moseley, leader of the British Union of Fascists, and many of his followers were arrested and jailed. So was Captain Ramsay, a member of Parliament, who was known to have anti-Jewish views like those of the Nazis. Members of the Irish Republican Army (IRA) who had been reckless enough to explode bombs in Britain at the outbreak of war were also imprisoned. It was as well that they were, for such was the temper of the British public that the members of the IRA would have been lynched had they been caught.

Everybody from terrorists to titled men fell into the

tightening security net. Admiral Sir Barry Domville was among the latter, for although at one time he had been chief of Naval Intelligence, he had also been chairman of an Anglo-German society called the Link.

While all this was happening, the British national daily press was loudly demanding that all aliens should be returned to their own countries for the security of Britain. This was a period of great tragedy for the 60,000 Germans, German Jews, and Austrians who, although they had fled from Nazism to save their lives, were still the objects of hatred and suspicion in Britain. There were also some 8,000 Czech refugees.

All these aliens were ruthlessly screened by special tribunals and classified into three groups; A, B, and C. Those in Group A were immediately interned; those in Group B were subjected to restriction of movement; and those of Group C were allowed to go free.

Some 4,000 Italians, mostly hotel and restaurant keepers and waiters who had lived less than 20 years in Britain, were also interned in spite of the fact that a number of them were refugees from Fascist Italy. It seems probable that some of these unfortunate Italians felt safer in the internment camps, for already a number of Italian-owned and managed hotels and restaurants had been wrecked by angry and frustrated Britons.

Towards the end of 1940, the internment measures grew more severe. Police chiefs were told to arrest any of the Group C aliens who seemed doubtful, and shortly after this all Class C aliens were arrested and interned. Invalids and key workers in industry were supposed to have been excluded from these internments, but it was not always so. The ruthless but necessary internment measures continued until very few aliens retained their liberty. Most of those who did were under curfew and were denied the use of bicycles and automobiles, and their movements were rigidly restricted.

The plan was to move the thousands of internees to the Isle of Man, from whence they would be deported overseas to the British Dominions and thus would not constitute a threat to British security. The aliens were moved to a number of transit camps, where, in some instances, the conditions were so bad as to be nearly barbarous. The aliens slept on the ground in tents, for there was no bedding and few blankets. They were sent to derelict buildings with little food and scant medical supplies.

Aliens were also denied radio sets, newspapers, and books; and a harsh censorship of mail was imposed on them. Worst of all, families were separated from each other; so it is not surprising that many of these war victims committed suicide.

These tragedies were sad enough, but even worse was to follow when the *Arandora Star* was torpedoed by an enemy submarine off the west coast of Ireland. This steamship was carrying 1,500 German and Italian internees to Canada, and among the many who died were German refugees to Britain who had been the bitter personal enemies of Adolf Hitler.

So desperate was the plight of aliens in Britain at that time that the famous author H. G. Wells was constrained to write a public letter condemning their treatment by the government. Nevertheless, the situation is understandable, for at this terrible moment in her history Britain faced the Nazis without and the threat of the dreaded fifth column within, and the presence of thousands of aliens added immeasurably to the latter peril.

The fifth column, which had already played a massive part in the overthrow of Belgium and Holland, cast such a shadow of dread over Britain that the country virtually became a police state, although the British public did not know it at the time. Letters were opened by the censor; telephone censors listened to telephone conversations; wherever people assembled in groups, their conversations were written down and reported. The BBC reported comments of their listeners, public figures reported the conversations of lesser people to the Ministry of Information, and the police watched and reported everybody.

The feeling was in the air that if Britain fell, it would more likely be the work of the fifth column from within than from invasion. To aggravate this terrible situation, the workers were saying bitterly among themselves that if Britain did collapse, then the rich and the privileged would flee the country, leaving them to face the Nazis alone. And rumor was abroad that the Royal Family had already gone to Canada.

William Joyce, a renegade of British-American-Irish ancestry known as Lord Haw Haw, who broadcast Nazi propaganda to Britain, was swift to exploit this situation. When 6,000 children were evacuated from Britain to America in the summer of 1940, Lord Haw Haw said in one of his broadcasts that these were the children of rich people. It was then that Winston Churchill gave this traitorous renegade a figurative, but nonetheless hard, slap in the mouth. He stopped his niece Sally Churchill from sailing to America, but even so Churchill himself recognized the possibility of defeat and saw to it that the gold reserves of Britain were shipped to Canada for safekeeping.

What added so immeasurably to the menace of Lord

Haw Haw was the fact that he *did* have his informants in Britain. This was proved when he made such radio announcements as declaring the time discrepancies of the clocks on town halls and in the public places of Britain. Also, he advised that it would be useless to enlarge the premises of certain factories, which he named and which actually were being extended, as they would be bombed anyway.

Sometimes his threats came to pass. For example, at the beginning of the war, he announced that English lightships on the east coast would be attacked and sunk. Nobody believed this, not even the lightships' crews, for the lightships were under the protection of the Geneva Convention, but Lord Haw Haw's threat was no idle one.

His efforts to dismay and so defeat the British were furthered by the activities of secret pro-Nazi organizations in Britain such as the New British Broadcasting Station, which threw suspicion on coal miners by broadcasting a statement that invading German paratroopers would be dressed like coal miners.

Another such pro-Nazi group, Workers' Challenge, had a secret radio station, which broadcast sedition and attempted to ferment industrial strife.

To counter this flood of enemy propaganda the BBC inaugurated a program called "Postscripts," in which the famous author J. B. Priestley broadcast anti-Nazi propaganda. Later he was succeeded in this work by the well-known American journalist Quentin Reynolds.

But the time was soon coming when the battle of words was to erupt into the Battle of Britain.

5. The Battle of Britain Commences

On June 14, 1940, the triumphant Nazis occupied Paris, and on June 17 France surrendered. The French government, now led by the aged Marshal Petain, asked for an armistice.

On June 18 Winston Churchill addressed the tense and silent members of the House of Commons. "What General Weygand called 'The Battle of France' is over," he told the members. "I expect the Battle of Britain to begin."

It is astonishing indeed to consider the fact that the overconfident Germans did not think this way at all, for on the same day that Churchill addressed the members of the British Parliament, Adolf Hitler said to Hermann Goering, chief of the Luftwaffe, "The war is over, Hermann. I am going to reach an agreement with England." And Hitler really believed that the war would soon be over, for he had said to Halder, his Chief of Staff, "England's resolve is weakening, believe me." From the very beginning, Hitler had shown apparent reluctance to attack Britain at all. He wanted Britain to play a leading part in the Nazi "New Order" for Europe, with the duke of Windsor on the throne of Britain as a puppet king and David Lloyd George as puppet prime minister.

Speaking with apparent sincerity at the Reichstag on July 19, 1940, Hitler said, "At this hour I feel it is my duty to appeal once more in good faith for reason and wise counsel on the part of Great Britain as of all other countries. I consider that my position allows me to make this appeal since I do not speak as a defeated man but as a victor speaking in the name of reason. I really see no reason why this war should continue. . . . Mr. Churchill ought, for once, to believe me when I say that a great empire will be destroyed—an empire it was never my intention to harm or destroy."

A soldier of the British Regiment of Guards, fresh from Dunkirk, was punished for saying of Winston Churchill while on parade, "He's a real fighter—the old bastard." If Winston Churchill had been less of a fighter and more of a conventional politician, he might have believed Hitler's honeyed words and sent Britain down into the darkness forever.

The only answer Hitler received was the continuously stiffening resistance of the British people. The combat planes of the Royal Air Force were already engaging the Luftwaffe in the opening stages of a battle that was to decide the fate of Britain and, ultimately, of the Third Reich.

During the warm, fine month of July, 1940, RAF Fighter Command flew 571 missions, although only seven enemy aircraft were destroyed for the loss of six British planes. Realizing that his blandishments were useless,

Hitler, in his order of the day of August 1, 1940, said, "I have decided that war against Great Britain will be pursued and intensified by sea and air with the object of bringing about that country's final defeat."

Hitler's plan was threefold: to destroy the Royal Air Force; to attack Britain's ports and food depots, especially those that supplied London; and to destroy the Royal and Merchant navies. The invasion of Britain under the code name *Seelöwe* ("sea lion") was fixed for September 11, 1940. To accomplish the invasion, Brauchitsch, the Nazi commander in chief, declared that it would be necessary for the German navy to land 40 divisions in Britain without loss. The Chiefs of Staff of the German navy told Brauchitsch frankly that they could only be responsible for ten divisions.

And while the Chiefs of Staff of the German army and navy haggled over the invasion, Britain was facing the massing might of the Luftwaffe, whose Second and Third Air Fleets were assembling on the Channel coasts of France. At this period the Royal Air Force had 650 aircraft under the command of Air Chief Marshal Sir Hugh Dowding.

The Luftwaffe had some 2,600 aircraft under Generals Kesselring and Sperrl, while in occupied Norway an additional 190 aircraft could be called upon if necessary. The Royal Air Force was outnumbered by more than four planes to one. Nor was this their only disadvantage. Adolf Galland, the brilliant Nazi "Fighter General" and his formidable Condor Legion had gained valuable combat experience during the Spanish civil war. In addition, the German fighter and bomber plane pilots and crews had received combat experience during the invasions of Poland, Holland, France, Belgium, and Norway. The only combat experience the British pilots had received was during their brief encounters with the enemy in France.

In comparing the aircraft of the opponents, the British Hurricane combat plane was considered equal in performance to the German Messerschmitt 110, but inferior to the formidable Messerschmitt 109, which was regarded as equal to the famous British Spitfire.

At this hazardous period the British combat plane pilots, whose life expectancy was calculated to be 87 hours in the air, were regarded as even more valuable than the planes they flew; for combat planes could be replaced faster than pilots could be trained.

To smash the massive Luftwaffe attacks that would make the invasion of Britain possible, Sir Hugh Dowding had to provide adequate air cover for the whole of Britain with four groups of combat planes. These were No. 10 Group, commanded by Air Vice-Marshal Sir C. J. Quintin Brand, with its headquarters at Box in the county of Wiltshire; No. 11 Group, commanded by Air Vice-Marshal Sir Rodney Park, with its headquarters at Uxbridge in the county of Middlesex; No. 12 Group, commanded by Air Vice-Marshal Sir Trafford Leigh Mallory, with headquarters at Watnall in the county of Nottinghamshire; and No. 13 Group, commanded by Air Vice-Marshal R. E. Saul, with its headquarters at Newcastle-upon-Tyne. These four groups comprised a total of 58 squadrons, four of which were nonoperative.

To support these groups, there were batteries of antiaircraft guns, searchlights, and balloon barrages around all the major cities, towns, and ports. Tellers of the Royal Observer Corps, posted at strategic points, reported the number, position, course, and estimated height of the enemy aircraft.

A network of radio detection and ranging stations (christened *radar* by the Americans, a name thereafter adopted for general usage) along the southern and southeastern coasts enabled Fighter Command to see the approaching enemy aircraft, giving the British planes time to take off and engage the enemy.

In the various Fighter Command Operations Rooms, known as Ops Rooms, a fighter controller kept in constant communication with the squadron leaders, directing them on their predetermined courses and heights until they engaged the enemy. Then they were on their own, for better for worse; for living or dying.

In the Ops rooms a new and terrible ordeal of war was endured by the young women of Britain's Women's Auxiliary Air Force (WAAFS), who had to move the colored counters representing the various RAF squadrons on large maps. There was direct radio contact with all combat plane pilots, whose individual voices could be heard over the speaker systems of the Ops Rooms.

From these speakers the young women of the WAAF, some of them hardly more than high school girls and most of whom had led sheltered and quiet lives, heard for themselves the fury, horror, and tragedy of battle in the air. They heard the voices of young men, many of whom they knew personally, shouting as they were locked in combat with the enemy. These young women heard the obscenities, the blasphemies, the terror, the rage; the triumphant victories or the violent deaths amid the endless screaming roar of engines and the tearing blast of machine gun fire.

Senior officers wanted to replace these shocked, pale-faced, and tearful girls. But the girls refused to be replaced and stayed to become quiet, stony-faced croupiers of death, pushing the colored counters across the maps.

Between July 10 and 24, 1940, when the Battle of Britain really began, the Luftwaffe had carried out more or less continuous attacks against the ships of the Royal Navy and British coastal merchant ships with JU 87 dive bombers (Stukas) by day and with Heinkel mine-laying aircraft by night. The new type of magnetic, and later acoustic, mines dropped by the Heinkels were detonated in the first instance by the magnetic attraction of the ship's hull and in the second instance by the sound impulses from the ship's engines and propellers. The explosions of these mines were so devastating they could blow a 3,000-ton coastal freighter so far out of the water that daylight could be seen along the entire keel.

This attack on British coastal shipping was part of Hermann Goering's plan to gain command of the English Channel by luring out and destroying as many RAF combat planes as possible. At first the pilots of the RAF combat planes found the Stukas very easy to deal with. "A piece of cake," they said, for the Stukas made easy targets when they dived to release their bombs or climbed after having released them.

The Luftwaffe swiftly remedied this by having an ME 109 combat plane follow each Stuka down and wait for the RAF combat planes to attack as the Stuka climbed again, free of its bomb load. These tactics paid off, for on August 8, 1940, 20 British combat planes were shot down in a three-wave Stuka attack on a large convoy of British merchant ships.

Another factor in favor of the Germans at this time was that their air-sea rescue services of fast motorboats, operating from the French coast, were far superior to the British rescue service. Most of the German pilots who had to bail out over the English Channel were saved, but unless a British pilot was lucky, he was lost.

Moreover, right from the very beginning, the RAF airfields in the exposed southeast corner of England were heavily attacked. Manston Airfield, near the seaside resort of Ramsgate, Kent, headquarters of the 600 City of London Squadron of Blenheim bombers and also of the famous No. 65 Fighter Squadron, was a priority target from the beginning. It was from Manston that the famous South African air ace Sailor Malan had taken off in his Spitfire to destroy many enemy aircraft, and possibly this was one of the reasons for its continued blasting by the enemy. Manston was, in fact, almost blasted out of existence. The airfield telephone systems were destroyed, hangars wrecked, many personnel killed and wounded, and the airfield so pitted with bomb craters that it resembled the surface of the moon in miniature. To make the scene even more terrifying, a fine haze of chalk dust hung perpetually over the airfield, settling on everything and making the hard-pressed surviving personnel look like ghosts.

Enemy bombers swept in over Hawkinge Airfield in Kent, destroying four aircraft on the ground; blasting hangars, workshops, and accommodation huts; and killing and wounding many personnel. During this raid a sergeant pilot of the RAF, who had been awarded the Distinguished Flying Medal and Bar for shooting down 14 enemy aircraft, went berserk when he saw his beloved Spitfire blown to pieces on the ground. Racing through the carnage of blazing planes and buildings, exploding ammunition, and smoking bomb craters, he leaped into a Spitfire that stood with its engine running and took off at full throttle after the bomber he had seen destroy his own Spitfire. The fact

that the plane he had grabbed belonged to his commanding officer did not worry him in the least. He wanted to
avenge his plane. And avenge it he did, for he caught up
with the bomber responsible, got it in his sights, and with a
prolonged blast from his eight machine guns sent the
offending bomber hurtling down in flames. It was his
fifteenth victory.

On August 16, 1940, airfields in the counties of Kent
(including famous Biggin Hill), Sussex, Hampshire, Essex,
and Suffolk were attacked. The towns of Worcester,
Chester, Tavistock in Devon, Farnborough in Hampshire,
Bristol, Newport, and Portland were also bombed.

Now the skies over Britain were a raging inferno of
noise, destruction, and death; and awful debris came tum-
bling down to earth. Whole planes and fragments of
planes screamed earthwards; parachutes and fragments of
parachutes came drifting down, as did corpses and fragments of corpses.

Between August 12 and August 17, 1940, the Nazis
claimed to have attacked 47 airfields and to have completely destroyed 11. The truth was that no British airfield was completely destroyed, not even Manston, the
most heavily and continuously attacked. Yet the Germans
claimed not only to have destroyed Manston Airfield, but
also No. 65 Fighter Squadron. This lie proved to be an
embarrassment for the Nazis, for every time thereafter
that they engaged No. 65 Squadron, they had to report
officially that they had destroyed it.

In addition to their all-out efforts to destroy British
airfields and so ground RAF Fighter Command, the Nazis
made determined efforts to destroy Britain's vital radar
stations. The radar station at Dover, where the tall, steel,

latticework towers still stand, could easily be seen by the Luftwaffe Chiefs of Staff across the Channel on a clear day. Oberleutnant Hintz of the Luftwaffe made frantic attempts to topple those slender steel towers that guarded Britain as mighty Dover Castle had guarded it in ancient times. But thanks to their latticework construction, the towers were largely proof against bomb blast, and a direct hit was never scored on them.

The radar station at Rye in the county of Sussex was not so fortunate, for it was hit and badly damaged by bombs. But it was swiftly repaired and operational again a mere three hours after the attack.

The only radar station in the whole of Britain to be completely destroyed by the Luftwaffe was at Ventnor on the Isle of Wight off the south coast of England.

On August 18, 1940, Lieutenant Lamberty of the Luftwaffe, in an attempt to evade Britain's radar network, led a squadron of nine Dornier bombers across the Channel, flying at only 100 feet to avoid radar detection. His objective was the all-important airfield at Biggin Hill, Kent. Here Lamberty's squadron encountered a new British antiaircraft device for the first time. It was the simple but deadly parachute and cable rocket (PAC rocket), invented by the Schermuly brothers, who before the war manufactured lifesaving rockets and flares. The new device was simply a rocket, fired from a line-throwing pistol and later from electrically operated batteries, which carried a small parachute attached to 400 feet of thin piano wire. Fired directly into the paths of attacking bombers, this rocket proved to be a very deadly weapon indeed, to which Stukas were extremely vulnerable.

As Lamberty's squadron roared over Biggin Hill, it

flew directly into a barrage of PAC rockets. Lamberty saw one of his Dorniers fly straight into a wire suspended from a small parachute and crash immediately. The next moment the wing of his own bomber was sliced away like cheese by one of the deadly floating wires. The bomber then burst into flames and Lamberty, already badly burned, managed to claw his way out of the melting cockpit with a badly burned member of his crew. As they landed by parachute, a squad of grim-faced Home Guardsmen closed in on them, rifles pointed and fingers tensed around triggers.

Most likely, Lamberty would have been shot on the spot, but as he raised his hands in surrender, the men of the Home Guard saw the flesh falling in strips from his roasted hands, and the sight made them lower their rifles. Lamberty then asked one of the Home Guard if he would get a packet of cigarettes from his still smoldering tunic. After the Home Guard had lit the cigarette, Lamberty, apparently unaware of his terrible burns, said in English, "What makes me really sad is that I think it will be a long a long time before I fly again."

As he spoke, another wave of Dornier bombers, escorted by ME 109 combat planes, roared in to hit Biggin Hill Airfield with more than a hundred bombs.

The two captured Germans and their Home Guard captors barely had time to throw themselves flat before the airfield was swept by a hurricane blast of flame, smoke, and screaming metal fragments.

This second wave of low-level Dorniers was so savagely mauled by ground fire and British combat planes that only two bombers escaped to stagger back to their base in occupied France. The pilot of one of the surviving

Dorniers had been killed, and the plane was flown back by a flight engineer who received the Iron Cross for his feat. Nobody, not even the British, could deny the fact that the Luftwaffe pilots were courageous and implacable.

In the meantime, seven Hurricanes of RAF 501 Squadron were engaged with 50 German bombers and their fighter escort planes near Hawkinge Airfield in Kent. The Hurricanes were outnumbered seven to one, but it made no difference, for they tore the enemy formation to shreds.

Wave after wave of Nazi bombers thundered remorselessly in over the eastern and southeastern coasts of England. Over the marshlands of eastern England, near the town of Chelmsford, Essex, planes of No. 85 Fighter Squadron, RAF, swooped like falcons on a massive enemy formation of bombers and combat planes that the Nazis called a Valhalla. This was an apt description, but not in the way the Germans meant, for in Old Norse *Valhalla* means "halls of the slain."

The Valhalla consisted of swarms of Stukas, protected by Heinkel bombers flying at 2,000 feet above them. Above the Heinkels thundered a formidable concentration of Junkers JU 88 bombers with an escort of many ME 100 combat planes. Over all flew an "umbrella" of the deadly ME 109s.

It was a sight to daunt the most valiant heart, but it did not daunt Flight Lieutenant Peter Townsend, who later wrote about his war experiences in *Duel of Eagles*. He swept into the attack, leading Red Section of RAF Fighter Command, with Flight Lieutenant Hemingway leading Blue Section. With them went Yellow and Green sections.

As the British planes attacked the complex formations of the Valhalla, it broke formation. The vulnerable Stukas turned back out to sea, while the JU 88 and Heinkel bombers circled protectively above them. Above the JU 88s and Heinkels, the ME 110s and ME 109s circled in their turn. It was an aerial "Wagon Train" attack, with the British pilots cast in the role of Indians.

The sky, crisscrossed with a web of white vapor trails, shook to the thunder of engines and battle as the diving, wheeling planes blasted away at each other. At last the Valhalla was dispersed with the loss of one Heinkel bomber, six ME 110s, and three ME 109s. The British lost two Hurricanes, with a third badly damaged.

Fighter Command of the RAF was attacking the Luftwaffe with a dedicated ferocity that had to be seen to be believed. Yet although it was inflicting massive losses on the enemy, the slender resources of the RAF, already dangerously stretched, were being whittled away.

Over the ten days between August 8 and 18 of 1940, the RAF lost 240 planes in the air and 30 on the ground, with 94 pilots killed or missing.

Over those ten days the British losses were heavy, but the German losses were appalling, for in that same period they lost 700 aircraft, and the whole of southeastern England was littered with the smoking wrecks of Nazi planes. To this day, storms along the eastern, southeastern, and southern coasts of England cast ashore the torn and bullet-riddled fragments of the aircraft that crashed into the sea during those ten terrible days.

Britain had dealt the mighty Third Reich a devastating blow in this first round of the battle for her survival. On August 20, 1940, Winston Churchill said to the packed and breathlessly waiting members of the House of Commons, "The gratitude of every home in our Island, in our Empire and indeed throughout the world except in the abodes of the guilty, goes out to British airmen who, undaunted by odds, unwearied in their constant challenge and mortal danger, are turning the tide by their prowess and their devotion. Never in the field of human conflict was so much owed by so many to so few."

Hermann Goering, chief of the Luftwaffe, was less pleased with his airmen. "They said a few days would be enough!" he shouted. "That's what they said at the beginning of the battle. Well now they had better start winning it!"

General Von Richthofen wrote in his journal: "We have to change our tactics and attack Britain with redoubled energy." But it was not that simple, for both the Chiefs of Staff of the RAF and of the Luftwaffe realized that they could not throw away planes and the lives of pilots as furiously as had been done in the first round of the Battle of Britain.

So, towards the end of August, 1940, the second round of the battle commenced more cautiously, and it was at this phase that the bombing of British towns and cities began.

At this time the war in the air reached another crucial stage. The German pilots who had been instructed to bomb Thames Haven oil refining plant near the mouth of the Thames dropped their bombs on London instead and among other destruction gutted the ancient church of St. Giles at Cripplegate. It is believed that this bombing was due to an error of navigation or perhaps panic, for up to this time German pilots had been instructed to bomb targets of military value only. Whatever the reason, Hermann Goering was furiously angry when he heard that London had been bombed. He demanded a complete report of the incident with the names of the pilots responsible, threatening that they would be disciplined and sent to infantry regiments as punishment.

Up to this period British bombers had only dropped propaganda leaflets on Berlin, but on August 25 Squadron Leader Oxley took off with a squadron of 81 twin-engine Hampden bombers to bomb the Seimens-Halske factory in Berlin. The British bombers encountered a heavy concentration of flak and, further hampered by low clouds, could not find their target. As the German pilots had, for one reason or another, bombed London, so did the British pilots drop their bomb loads on Berlin.

After the bombing, Adolf Hitler, in one of his fearful frenzies, screamed to a rally of women social workers and nurses in Berlin, "When the British air force drops two or three or four thousand kilograms of bombs, we in one night will drop one hundred and fifty, two hundred and thirty, three hundred, or four hundred thousand kilograms. When they declare they will increase their attacks on our cities, we will raze their cities to the ground. We will stop the work of these night air pirates, so help us God!"

The women gave their führer a standing ovation, but they could not see then that the Nazis had sown the wind and the Germans would reap the awful whirlwind in the fire tempests that incinerated Hamburg and Dresden and tens of thousands of their townsfolk.

Hitler's speech, however, did little to restore the dwindling prestige of the Luftwaffe, whose planes the RAF had hammered from the skies of Britain. German pilots were spat on in the streets of towns and cities, and even Goering himself was publicly abused by angry Berliners, whom he had once told confidently that their city would never be bombed.

Yet in spite of Hitler's speech to the women of Berlin and the loss of his own prestige, Goering was still unwilling to bomb British towns and cities. His motives were not humanitarian ones, for he firmly believed, and history has proved him right, that only by destroying RAF Fighter Command could Britain be invaded and at last defeated. Notwithstanding his own convictions, Goering gave way to the wishes of Adolf Hitler and announced that reprisals for the bombing of Berlin would be taken. In his decision to bomb the towns and cities of Britain, Goering did not take into consideration the implacable character of Sir Hugh Dowding, who he thought would sacrifice the combat planes of Fighter Command to protect those towns and cities.

Nearly 19 centuries before the Battle of Britain, the iron-willed Roman general, Suetonius Paulinus, had sacrificed London and its citizens to the raging hordes of the rebel tribes of the Iceni. He did this to preserve his legions, so that they in turn could save the rest of Roman Britain from the rebels.

Sir Hugh Dowding was equally resolved to sacrifice London and its citizens to the Luftwaffe, if necessary, in order to preserve the vital Fighter Command, upon which the fate of Britain and its empire depended.

Even so, the attack by 207 German bombers with fighter escort on London on the night of September 7, 1940, caught Fighter Command unprepared. The dockland areas of East End of London were the targets upon which rained tens upon tens of thousands of 1-kg electron incendiary bombs, 350 mm long and 50 mm in diameter. The cases of these small but devastating bombs were of aluminum alloy mixed with 90 percent magnesium, which melted at 650 degrees and burned like the fires of hell.

Jets of water only caused these bombs to crackle and blaze more fiercely, and they could only be extinguished by a fine spray of water from stirrup pumps or by being buried in sand or earth or smothered by sandbags. Handling them, even with the long-handled shovels used by the ARP, could be very dangerous. Many of the incendiary bombs had additional hazards in the form of charges of electron thermite, making them almost as lethal as grenades or mortar bombs. After the hissing, whispering deluge of fire bombs came waves of German bombers which rained down high-explosive S.C. splinter bombs and 500-kg and 1000-kg bombs packed with TNT. The East End of London was ravaged by a hurricane of fire and blast that lasted without break from the night of September 7 until the dawn of September 8.

Watchers from the southern downlands 50 miles away saw a vast, flickering, red dome in the sky. Into that fiery dome stick after stick of high-explosive bombs howled and shrieked, adding to the death, destruction, and horror. The endless deluge of bombs hurled the flaming debris up like a burning tidal wave, swamping rescuers and rescued, doctors and nurses, firemen and police, ambulance men and ARP personnel in a sea of flame and horror. There were no longer any streets or houses, only blazing funeral pyres and mounds of smoking rubble, which covered the dead and the fragments of the dead.

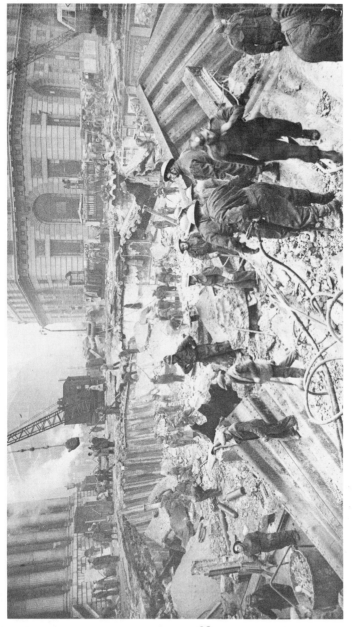

Bomb damage at Bank Station, London. *Courtesy of London Transport Board*

83

Flames roared from shattered gas mains and water from smashed uprooted water mains, where firemen paused to extinguish their smoldering uniforms before taking their pumps perilously to the muddy Thames. Telephone wires were cut, so that rescue parties (firemen, police, doctors, ARP workers, and others) had to use runners to take messages of each fresh incident, along the awful places where the streets had been, to the various control rooms and hospitals.

It was the men of the fire service, once despised as draft dodgers, who were now the heroes of the awful hour, running their endless miles of hoses across mounds of rubble and layers of shattered glass and twisted steel and through flame amid a howling deluge of death from the sky.

In times of peace, a fire that rated the attendance of ten fire pumps was termed a conflagration, meaning "a great and destructive fire." On the early morning of September 8, 1940, there were nine raging holocausts in The East End of London, each one rating 100 fire pumps; 19 fires, rating 30 fire pumps each; 40 fires, rating ten fire pumps each; and over a thousand comparatively minor blazes.

In the Surrey Docks the firemen tried to quench a Gargantuan bonfire of 200 acres of stacked dry timber. In the ruins of the bonded warehouses of the docks, thousands of barrels of bonded liquor exploded like bombs, and the blazing liquor ran in rivers of blue flame to mingle with streams of gurgling, blazing molasses from a factory. Crates of pepper from other warehouses exploded in the superheated atmosphere, filling the unbreathable air with rolling, choking clouds of stinging dust, causing frenzies of sneezing and retching and blinding the firemen who vainly tried to exorcise the raging fire demon.

A sea of melted rubber in a burning warehouse filled the air with choking black smoke and leaping orange flames. Streams of blazing paint and varnish gushed from another gutted warehouse, choking the nearby fire pumps in a sticky, white-hot torrent.

It was almost impossible to breathe in the superheated air, and many people were stifled to death. Firemen, almost embalmed in a foul and clinging mixture of greasy soot, oil, and water, found they could only breathe by thrusting their heat-skinned, grimy faces into the current of cool air caused by the gush of water from their hoses.

In the same way that forest fire fighters are sometimes surrounded by flames and perish, so perished firemen in the second Great Fire of London.

ARP workers, heavy and light rescue squads, ambulance crews, policemen, firemen, anybody who was in the blazing hell of London's dockland, had but one objective —to get the living out of the ruins. They dug like demented badgers, sometimes with their bare hands, in the smoking rubble and brickwork that had once been small, terraced houses. The dead were left buried, for it was only the living who mattered now.

Individual deeds of heroism were infinite, from the courage of a young office boy who sacrificed his life to save a nurse from falling masonry to the awesomely cold courage of Lieutenant Davies and Sapper Wylie of the Royal Engineers, who received the George Cross for working three days without break in a 25-foot-deep pit, defusing a bomb which, had it exploded, would have destroyed St. Paul's Cathedral.

In view of the torrent of fire and high explosive poured on London on that first night of the blitz, the casualty figures were astonishingly light. There were 430 people killed and 1,600 seriously injured.

The next morning Winston Churchill and Mr. Harold Scott, chief of London's Civil Defence, visited London's ravaged East End. Though it was early in the day, the people who had survived were already carrying their bedding and personal possessions to the deep underground tunnels of London's tube train network. Shocked and exhausted as they were, they stopped and cheered when they saw Churchill being driven through the rubble, over a chaos of twisted fire hoses, broken glass, and debris.

Standing up amid the stench of burned high explosive, charred wet wood, burned rubber, paint—and death, Churchill held up his famous flat-crowned derby hat on his walking stick to those who cheered him. "Are we downhearted?" he shouted.

"NO!" came back the roaring reply.

Britain's Old Bulldog wept openly and unashamedly at the undying courage and fortitude of these people he led.

As Churchill's car was being driven away, a time-fused bomb exploded, destroying a shop just ahead of the prime minister's automobile. Churchill just smiled, for he was still the same man who had charged with the British lancers at Omdurman.

On this first morning after the blitz of London, the code word *Cromwell*, which meant that invasion was imminent, was passed. Church bells were rung to warn the people; bridges were blown up; and the troops of the Home

Londoners take shelter in the Underground. *Courtesy of London Transport Board*

Forces, which included the men of the Home Guard and the Territorial Army, waited tensely for the attack.

The invasion did not come, but at 8:00 P.M. on September 9 the fleets of German bombers brought flaming hell to London again. Four hundred people died, and every main railway line in the south of England was temporarily put out of operation. Thereafter *for 76 consecutive nights*, with the exception of November 2, owing to adverse weather conditions, German bombers drenched London with incendiary and high-explosive bombs.

On the night of September 13, in spite of bad flying conditions, a group of German bombers slipped through the heavy clouds, their daring pilots determined to strike at the very heart of the Establishment of Britain. They bombed Buckingham Palace, badly damaging the Royal Chapel; blasted Downing Street, where stood No. 10, the official residence of Britain's prime minister; struck Whitehall, the center of Britain's administrative power; and damaged Trafalgar Square, where stands the statue of Admiral Sir Horatio Nelson, Britain's best loved hero of the past.

The Nazis justified the bombing of Buckingham Palace, Downing Street, Whitehall, and Trafalgar Square by saying that it was done in retaliation for the RAF's bombing of the Reichstag building, the Tiergarten, and the House of Engineers in Berlin. The Germans went to great lengths and made a number of accusations to justify their bombing of London. They accused Winston Churchill of deliberately ordering the RAF to bomb Germany's national monuments instead of military installations. They also accused him of ordering the RAF to drop sackfuls of live weevils on the grainfields of occupied Europe to destroy the harvest. Presumably, this accusation was made to justify the Germans' attempts to burn Britain's growing crops of wheat, oats, and barley by dropping incendiary bombs in the grainfields. These attempts failed because the grain crops were still green and would not ignite.

It is also probable that these increasingly hysterical accusations were prompted by the knowledge that the possibility of the successful invasion of Britain was becoming more and more remote.

Nevertheless, the entire British nation continued to brace itself for invasion and the code name *Cromwell* remained in operation for twelve days, with Britain's Home Forces poised to repel the enemy.

The normally pleasant and friendly beaches of eastern, southeastern, and southern England were dark and deadly places: desolate zones, which were a deadly maze of coiled barbed wire; bristling steel chevaux-de-frise to rip landing craft; and tens upon tens of thousands of hidden mines, numbers of which remain lost in remoter places to this day. Everywhere along the shores of England silent sentries stood with loaded rifles and fixed bayonets. And everywhere warning notices told people to keep off the beaches if they wished to live.

Some of those permitted to remain in the war zones for various reasons ignored these notices and still continued to wander along the beaches as they had done in peacetime. Quite a number were killed or injured by stepping on land mines.

"He's coming. He's coming," many of the British people said of Hitler as their ancestors had said of Napoleon. However, like the hordes of Napoleon, the million Nazi troops poised for the invasion of Britain did not come. The ferocious ability of RAF Fighter Command made Hitler think again. Obsessed with Nordic folklore and the themes of the great Wagnerian operas, the führer knew that it would be the Twilight of the Gods for his proud Third Reich if such an invasion were mounted and failed. Thus Hitler's Operation Sea Lion was postponed again while his navy, dubious of success against the powerful Royal Navy, made slow and unwilling preparations for the invasion.

Taking immediate advantage of this indecision, Bomber Command of the RAF continuously and remorselessly blasted the German invasion barges massed along the coasts of occupied France and Belgium.

On the nights of September 17 and 18, 1940, 268 German bombers attacked London again, this time bombing such famous and fashionable places as Oxford Street, Savile Row, and Bond Street. But British bombers, too, were thundering through the night; and their targets were not the fashion centers of Berlin, but the coasts, where the Germans were frantically massing a million men for the invasion of Britain, now scheduled for between September 15 and 21.

Like the fearful Bifrost Bridge of Norse legend, the occupied coasts of Belgium and France were one vast barrier of multicolored flame, intensified by the sudden incandescent glare of bursting bombs and the flak from German ground defenses. The Calais docks were one great sea of fire; so was Boulogne and the wide sweep of coast beyond it. Ostend cowered beneath a deluge of British

Above ground. *Courtesy of London Transport Board*

Below ground. *Courtesy of London Transport Board*

91

incendiary and high-explosive bombs. Beneath the hail of British bombs, the massed German invasion barges were blown to pieces and hurled up out of the flame-lit water, turning end over end as they went.

One British bomber flying at 4,000 feet was suddenly caught in a cosmic glare of light and buffeted through the air by a gigantic blast. The pilot said that his bomber flew through the air like an autumn leaf in a gale of wind, end over end. He was lucky to have survived, for later he learned that his entire bombload had scored a direct hit on a dump of 500 tons of mines waiting to be loaded into minelayers for the invasion of Britain. Aerial photographs of the vicinity of the mine dump showed that everything within a mile radius of the gigantic explosion had been pulverized.

While RAF Bomber Command was hammering Hitler's vaunted "Sea Lion" to death, RAF Fighter Command was busy smashing the Luftwaffe.

On September 18, Britain's famous legless air ace, Squadron Leader Douglas Bader, supported by the famous Polish pilot Satchell and his Fighting Poles, smashed 19 German planes from the sky without loss to themselves. On the night of September 19 to 20, the Germans retaliated with a deluge of bombs from 123 bombers, which tore London apart from 9:00 P.M. onwards. Watchers said that approaching London was like approaching Dante's Inferno.

Hitler, in the meantime, had ordered Admiral Raeder to disperse what remained of the badly mauled invasion fleet along the Belgian and French coasts in order to minimize the destruction it was suffering from the remorseless raids of RAF Bomber Command.

The possibility of the German invasion of Britain was receding, but at the same time the bombing of the two opposing capital cities, London and Berlin, intensified. Although London had the worst of this exchange of blows, the Luftwaffe paid a deadly price for its attacks.

On September 27, a massed formation of German bombers with combat plane escort, droned towards London. It was the last of their vaunted Valhallas and never was the sinister meaning of that name more appropriate for the Nazi pilots.

In a mesh of white vapor trails and to the tearing rip of prolonged machine gun and cannon fire, the fury of RAF Fighter Command smashed down from the misty sunshine over the county of Kent like the lightning hammer of Thor.

In the words of Squadron Leader Deacon Elliot of Squadron 72, "The German bombers were literally massacred. Their escort would not come down to fight, and I doubt if a single one reached home."

That day all the Ops Rooms of Fighter Command resounded to the blast of machine gun and cannon fire and the jubilant cries of "Tallyho" from young British pilots, some only in their teens, as they hunted down the enemy as their sporting ancestors had hunted foxes. Forty-five German planes went down in smoke and flames into the cold gray green waters of the English Channel, and the sea was foul with the debris of shattered Nazi planes and the dead bodies of German aircrews. Twenty-eight British planes were shot down, the majority of them falling on the land.

The next day RAF Fighter Command received this message from Winston Churchill:

Pray congratulate Fighter Command on the results of yesterday. The scale and intensity of the fighting and the heavy losses to the enemy make September 27 rank with September 15th and August 15th as the third great victorious day of Fighter Command during the Battle of Britain.

The losses suffered by the Luftwaffe were crippling beyond redemption, for from the end of July to November 4, 1940, a total of 96 days, the enemy lost the staggering number of 2,224 aircraft. Even the mighty Luftwaffe could not sustain such losses as this, and so they lost the Battle of Britain. But as Air Marshal Sir Hugh Dowding, who was made Grand Companion of the Order of the Bath for his services to Britain, wrote later: "If the Fighter Defence had failed in the autumn of 1940 England would have been invaded."

With the threat of invasion lifted from Britain, the conflict was now to become a war of attrition.

6. The Blitz in London and the Provinces

For the moment, the Royal Air Force had destroyed Germany's hopes of invasion and given besieged Britain time to draw breath for the next onslaught from the air.

The towns and cities of Britain lay exposed to the bombers of the Luftwaffe; and from September, 1940, until May, 1941, the British public, especially the citizens of London, endured hell on earth. Those who at first had left the towns for the country and then returned to the towns had long escaped to the safety of the countryside again, at least those fortunate or wealthy enough to be able to do so. The majority of the British people whose work or commitments forced them to remain in the towns and cities had to endure a nightly ordeal of noise, destruction, and death.

The terror of those night raids is still vivid to those who remember them. When the ominous, undulating wail of the warning sirens had died, one listened for the distant drone of massed bombers, a drone that swiftly became a terrifying, throbbing roar as they flew directly overhead.

Then came the whistle and shriek of falling bombs; the roar and cyclone blast of the explosions; the shattering of glass; the rumble of collapsing houses and buildings; the shrieks of the injured, the dying, and the demented.

The perpetual and sibilant whisper of falling incendiary bombs was followed by the crackle and roar of the fires they spread. Added to this was the wracking blast of antiaircraft guns and rocket batteries, the lethal hail of flak splinters and shell nose caps and sometimes unexploded shells, which inevitably added to the nightly quota of civilian casualties.

Edward R. Murrow, the American war correspondent, said, "The individual's reaction to the sound of falling bombs cannot be described. The moan of stark terror and suspense cannot be encompassed by words; no more can the sense of relief when you realize that you were not where that one fell."

Sometimes people were so paralyzed with fear that they had to be pushed or knocked over and dragged to cover—if there was time. But mostly the individual reaction had one aspect that was common to all. With held breath you listened to the screaming whistle and the "Crump . . . crump . . . crump!" of the falling bombs as they exploded. If the whistling and the "crumps" receded, then you just went on doing whatever it was. But if those awful sounds came closer, you dived for cover; if indoors, down the air raid shelter if it was near enough; if you were caught in the open, you would fall flat on your face with your hands locked over your head. You *fell flat* wherever you were or whatever you might fall flat into.

When a bomb fell really close and you were lucky enough to survive, the explosion would sometimes be beyond the compass of hearing. In such instances, you would feel the earth buckle and heave as if in an earthquake, and then would come the unendurable, searing heat of the blast. For a split second after, there would be a dreadful silence, then the thumping of falling masonry and debris, the screams and the cries and the demented howling of dogs.

In time, you learned to pay more attention to the behavior of dogs and cats than to the ARP wardens, for these animals were far more sensitive to danger than human beings. Sometimes for as much as half an hour before the arrival of the bombers, dogs would whimper, whine, howl, bark, and then tear off down the street or, if indoors, dive under chairs, tables, or beds.

Cats would just vanish like ghosts. The survival mechanism of cats seemed to be superior to that of dogs, who tended often to stay indoors with their owners and often die with them. Cats, on the other hand, tended to disappear and then come back unharmed to the pile of debris that had once been the house that sheltered them.

As the blitz continued, all but the very brave (or stupid), those whose work prevented it and those who were tired of life anyway, took to air raid shelters of one kind or another.

The most common type of air raid shelter to be seen in Britain was the Anderson shelter, two and a quarter million of which were provided free of charge to the public. This type consisted of curved sections of stout corrugated steel that were bolted to steel girders, the whole being then sunk into the earth to a minimum safety depth of three feet. The deeper the shelters were sunk, the greater safety they provided, except of course from a direct hit.

The earth from the excavation was then packed tightly over the top of the shelter, and a steel "blast door" with earth or sandbags piled against it was erected at the entrance, reached by going down a flight of small steps. The largest of these shelters could accommodate six people, who could sleep in wooden bunks erected against the walls. Oil, pressure gas lamps, or electric battery lamps provided light.

These Anderson shelters undoubtedly saved tens of thousands of lives, but they had their drawbacks nevertheless. In winter they were unbearably cold and saturated with condensation. This, together with the lack of proper ventilation, played havoc with the health of old people and those prone to such ills as bronchitis. Sometimes, too, the shelters became flooded and had to be bailed out before they could be used. If the shelters were not used regularly or kept closed, they became homes for innumerable stray dogs, cats, and even rats driven from their holes by the bombing.

The author, whose wife and baby daughter had been evacuated to the country, came home from sea for a few days; and although he lived at Sutton in Surrey on the outskirts of London, he decided that it would be safer to sleep in the Anderson shelter at the bottom of the garden.

During the night he felt something moving on his chest. Switching on the light, he peered with increasing dismay at a large and mangy rat sitting a few inches from his face and nonchalantly cleaning its whiskers. Too tired to worry about German bombers, the author surrendered the shelter to the rat and went upstairs intending to go to bed. Instead he spent the rest of the night bathing and getting rid of the fleas that stray dogs, cats, and rats had left in the shelter.

Anderson shelters, for all their disadvantages, were at least private places where a normal-sized family could be as comfortable as could be expected. In heavily built-up areas (where back gardens were nonexistent and Anderson shelters could not be erected), brick-built surface shelters for up to 50 people were provided. These were, frankly, quite horrible. Of such poor construction that they sometimes collapsed if a bomb fell anywhere near, they were dark, dank, and cold; and although provided with chemical lavatories, they stank to high heaven.

Smaller but much safer and infinitely more comfortable were the Morrison indoor shelters, named after Herbert Morrison, the minister of supply and later minister of home security. These shelters, called table shelters, consisted of strong steel plate tops that were supported by strong vertical steel girders and were about the height of a table, hence their name. Surrounded by stout steel wire mesh to keep out falling debris, they were capable of sustaining the entire weight of a normal house if it collapsed; and so, they saved many lives.

To a number of people, the word *shelter* had a rather more spiritual and social meaning than a literal one. Such people tended to shelter together in churches and assembly halls, gaining comfort from familiar, friendly faces, rather than from the strength or suitability of the structure they were in. With this type of shelterer it was a matter of "If we go—well, we all go together." Although this was touching and showed spiritual faith, such an attitude of mind gave no thought for the extra burden imposed on rescue services and medical helpers if the "shelter" received a hit or was demolished by blast.

In fact, any structures that just *seemed* safe were used as shelters. Among these were basements of buildings and cellars, where depth below ground gave the illusion of safety. People preferred to forget that even a relatively small 250-kg bomb could penetrate to a depth of 50 feet and that even if the structure was only demolished by blast, they would be entombed by the tons of rubble above them.

Undoubtedly, the worst of these places that gave the illusion of safety, but which in fact were deathtraps, were railway arches. The most infamous of these were Tilbury railway arches at Stepney in The East End of London, which had also been used as air raid shelters during World War I. These arches were taken over by the Stepney Borough Council as a public air raid shelter for 3,000 people and became the nightly abode of foreign seamen, prostitutes, and vagrants, who mingled with the other shelterers. The filth of this place and its packed humanity made it a focal point for morbid sightseers and war correspondents eager for pictures that emphasized the horrors of the London blitz.

Another shocking air raid shelter in the borough of Stepney was Mickey's Shelter, named after a hunchback dwarf, Mickey Davis, who made his permanent abode here. This vast celler was capable of sheltering 5,000 people, but it nightly sheltered nearer 10,000. So unbearable was the atmosphere here that people fainted by the score and had to be passed over the heads of the crowd and up into the fresh air to revive them.

Thanks to the tireless efforts of Mickey Davis and his

helpers, this shelter at last became clean and well organized. Eventually the board of directors of Marks and Spencer, the great chain stores, installed a modern canteen here; and Wendell Willkie, President Roosevelt's political rival, was shown Mickey's Shelter as a shining example of how modern democracy worked in wartime.

It was to be expected that air raid shelters in crowded slum areas should be grim and sometimes sordid and that air raid shelters for the public in prosperous upper and middle-class areas should be pleasant and comfortable.

In the pleasant, residential area, of Chiselhurst in Kent are the famous Chiselhurst Caves, once the abode of Stone Age man. Here, as they did in Ramsgate, Kent, several thousand people took over the well-ventilated, caves as a permanent residence for the duration of the blitz, setting up homes with beds, chairs, tables, cooking equipment, and other domestic appliances. Eventually, Chiselhurst Caves became the abode of a complete, well-organized underground community, served by special trains from London and even having its own concert parties and church services.

But it was to the network of tunnels of London's underground electric trains that the vast majority of Londoners went nightly to shelter from the blitz in spite of official fears that it would in time have an adverse psychological effect on the shelterers. Presumably the officials were fearful that a race of twentieth-century troglodytes would emerge at the end of the war. In addition to this, officialdom declared that the tubes had to be kept clear to permit troop movement should it be necessary. Londoners just ignored this official attitude, purchased ordinary platform tickets, and queued up nightly with their blankets, mattresses, and pillows for sleeping places on the platforms and, after the electrical power had been switched off at 10:30 p.m., even on the tracks amid the rails.

The tubes, which nightly provided shelter and comparative rest and comfort for Londoners, were unfortunately not proof against direct hits from bombs. An appalling incident occurred at Balham near London, when a bomb crashed through the road above the station and killed many of the 600 shelterers, 64 of whom were drowned in torrents from shattered water and effluent from sewage mains. A direct hit on the Bank Station in January, 1941, killed more than 100 people, and another direct hit on Marble Arch subway killed 20 people.

The citizens of London, however, undeterred by official disapproval and by direct hits from German bombs, continued to use the Underground stations and subways as air raid shelters. At last, officialdom bowed to the inevitable and gave way to the public, sanctioning the permanent use as shelters of disused Underground stations and unfinished extensions of the Underground lines.

The scenes below the streets of London at this time were like nothing the old city, or indeed the entire world, had ever witnessed before. At 10:30 p.m., when the trains had stopped running, the platforms of the stations were so tightly packed with sleepers that one could not even walk among them. People slept on the switched off moving stairs, in hammocks over the tracks, and on beds between the lines. There were no trains running in the unfinished extension of the Liverpool Street Line; so people were able to remain there permanently. Those families who had lost their homes by bombing or who preferred to live underground rather than in the incredibly dismal rest centers for the homeless, took up their abode here indefinitely.

Some of London's Underground tubes are very deep indeed, so deep that when one is traveling through them, one's eardrums pop owing to the increased pressure. Such deep tubes as these lay below the level of London's sewerage systems, so that there were no lavatories or toilet facilities available to the thousands of people who used them as air raid shelters. In time, this became a fearful health hazard, and medical statistics show that there was a marked increase in such "dirt diseases" as scabies and impetigo among the public who used these shelters. It might have been worse though, for these places might well have incubated the virulent typhus called the Black Death, which in the mid-fourteenth century destroyed million lives in Britain and Europe alone.

To supplement the tubes of London's Underground and public and private air raid shelters of every type, four great caverns were excavated beneath London to accommodate a total of 40,000 people. These, however, were not completed before the end of the blitz, although they later served as shelters from the V-2 rockets fired from France. They finally served as offices for General Eisenhower and his staff for the D-day invasion of Europe.

A considerable number of diehards refused to have any part of any type of air raid shelter. They would not put up with the health hazards, lack of privacy, general discomfort, and often misery of the air raid shelters. These would fill themselves with beer and spirits or, lacking alcohol, take sleeping pills, saying in a jovially fatalistic manner, "If my number is up, then I shan't know anything about it." Then they would go upstairs to bed and fall into a deep alcohol or drug-induced sleep, frequently slumbering on through heavy air raids and noise enough to wake the dead.

Night after night the blitz went on, and night after night the German bombers came droning and rumbling overhead, especially on clear, moonlit nights when targets were easy to identify.

In Norse mythology one encounters the legend of the Moon of Urd. This was an unusual aspect of the full moon, which the Norse peoples believed betokened death to many.

On clear, moonlit nights, people in Britain would look up at the cloudless sky, shake their heads, and say forebodingly, "It's a bomber's moon tonight." So the "bomber's moon" became part of the grim folklore of twentieth-century Britain.

At the beginning of the blitz, the German bombs weighed only 250 kg. but soon they weighed up to 2,500 kg. And from the very beginning, the German bombers had been dropping "Land mines" by parachute. These fearful missiles were, in fact, sea mines; black cylinders eight feet long and two feet in diameter and packed with devastatingly powerful high explosive. These would come floating down, the only sound being the wind in the parachute shrouds, to catch on church steeples, in tall trees, and on high buildings.

The heroic bomb disposal squads found these monstrosities difficult to deal with, and the general public feared them even more than bombs because of their shocking blast effect.

The blast of even a heavy bomb was often lessened to a degree by the fact that the bomb buried itself before exploding. But land mines exploded in the air or on the surface and the blast could be indescribably hellish and freakish. Blasts could hurl an entire train, engines and coaches, into the air like a toy or toss a man nearly half a mile, leaving him dead and unrecognizable or physically unharmed but stripped naked and shocked silly. A house could be destroyed with its occupants, but a pet canary left alive in an undamaged cage. Sometimes the sides of houses were sliced away as if by a giant razor, leaving contents and furnishing for all to see, like a giant dollhouse. People would be found dead, but unmarked, killed by blast where they huddled for shelter in shop doorways.

But perhaps most hellish and freakish of all were the things land-mine blast could do to glass. The plate glass windows of shops and business premises would distintegrate into huge, whistling, razor-edged fragments, which lopped heads, bodies, and limbs like the axes of demented executioners.

A quarter of a mile from the explosion, houses and buildings would be left standing, roofs stripped of tiles, but the glass of the windows driven inwards, leaving walls, furniture, and human bodies bristling with long glass "daggers" and looking like the targets of demon knife-throwers.

Night after night, the bombs, land mines, and incendiary bombs showered down on Britain. Night after night, civil defense workers, heavy and light rescue squads, fire departments, police, ambulance workers, air raid wardens, doctors, nurses, the gallant women of the WVS (Women's Voluntary Services), and the general public worked like furies to succor the victims of the blitz. They dug out the living victims from the piles of still smoking, perilously toppling ruins and rubble; tried to ease the dying and mutilated; tried to comfort the shocked, but physically unharmed, who in one traumatic instant had lost their dear ones and their homes; fought the flames and shored up the crumbling walls of bomb-blasted houses, buildings, and factories.

Shattered streets where broken gas mains flamed and smashed water mains gushed in the cratered roads would be sealed off with road diversion signs warning the public to keep out. Unexploded bombs, which were all too frequent and were called UXBs would be cordoned off to be dealt with by heroic bomb disposal experts; and the people who remained alive in the vicinity would be evacuated to relatives or rest centers.

When dust-shrouded, stinking dawn cast its gray light on the appalling scene, rubber-gloved, rubber-aproned civil defense workers who were chosen for their strong nerves and stomachs, would commence the ghastly task of collecting the human debris that lay scattered piecemeal everywhere. These dreadful but pathetic remnants were then taken to the mortuaries, where the attendants had an even more gruesome task than the "collectors." They had to make up bodies from the remnants for decent burial as best they could, and thus one body (?) was made up from all that was left of several victims.

Sometimes the victims were buried so far beneath the mountains of debris that their bodies were never found; and when these sites were cleared at last, a strange and spine-chilling thing was noticed: wherever people had been buried and left, the purple flowered shrub called buddleia grew and thrived. And so another grim twentieth-century legend was born of the blitz, for the innocent and beautiful buddleia was thereafter called the blood bush.

London endured the longest bombardment of any city in the history of the world and one that increased in ferocity and weight.

On the first 67 nights of the blitz, a nightly average of 160 bombers dropped 200 tons of high-explosive bombs and 180 canisters of incendiary bombs. For the last 19 nights of the blitz on London, a nightly average of 240 bombers dropped 290 tons of high-explosive bombs and 1,270 canisters of incendiary bombs. On the night of May 10, 1941, 3,000 people were killed or badly wounded in London, the main line railway services were put out of action for seven weeks, and the chamber of the House of Commons at Westminster was demolished. There were 2,000 fires, and the fact that a large number of water mains were destroyed at a time when the River Thames was at exceptionally low tide severely hampered the heroic work of the firemen.

Winston Churchill afterwards said that this was the most destructive raid of the entire blitz of London.

The British have been rightly described as an insular-minded people. It is quite astonishing to consider how this insularity of mind persisted in the provinces of Britain during the blitz on London. People in the provincial towns and cities tended to regard the bombing of London almost with complacency. To the intense frustration and often anger of Londoners who visited the provinces, they did not want to hear about it or discuss it. It seemed as if their attitude was: "If we don't talk about it, it won't happen to us."

But it did happen, suddenly and devastatingly.

By this time, the Germans had developed a form of bombing attack that was both simple and deadly. They sent a radio-directed force of Pathfinder bombers to drench a selected target with incendiary bombs and so provide a flaming beacon to guide further waves of bombers carrying high-explosive bombs.

On November 14, 1941, the ancient and beautiful city

of Coventry, with 213,000 inhabitants, was the first city in Britain to suffer this form of attack in a continuous bombardment that lasted for ten hours. The German bombers caught Coventry totally unprepared; and the Pathfinder bombers first drenched the ancient heart of the city with fire bombs, making an inferno of the old timbered houses and gutting the world-famous cathedral.

Guided by this beacon of destruction, German bombers deluged the city with hundreds of tons of high-explosive bombs. The attack was devastating; the ancient heart of the city was totally destroyed; nearly one-third of the city's houses were demolished, together with hundreds of shops. Railway lines were blocked, telegraph wires were cut, public transport was completely wrecked, 600 people were killed, and 900 were badly injured.

That single raid on Coventry had a more dire psychological effect on the citizens of Coventry than the entire blitz had had on the citizens of London. And this was understandable.

To begin with, London was a vast and sprawling city, a huge target that could not possibly be bombed all at once. The inhabitants of London had the tubes and other air raid shelters below ground to go to. Alternatively, they could flee to the sprawling suburbs, which were not being attacked.

The people of Coventry, on the other hand, lived in a relatively small and compact city, which rendered it an ideal target for concentrated bombing and which had few of the air raid shelter facilities of London.

It seemed to the suddenly demoralized citizens of Coventry that each whistling bomb was aimed directly at them individually. They had no safe place to go, only out

The smoke-stained, bomb-pitted shell of old Coventry Cathedral, partially restored after its destruction. *Courtesy of the*
Provost and Chapter of Coventry Cathedral

of the city altogether. So for the first time since the blitz on Britain started, shocked, dazed, and terror-stricken refugees, their faces black with soot and blank with shock, streamed from a ravaged city, which was hidden beneath a monstrous black pall of smoke. Every conceivable type of transport could be seen on the roads leading out of Coventry, everything from motortrucks to baby carriages and handcarts loaded with bedding and possessions. It was a sight tragically reminiscent of the roads of Flanders during the holocaust of World War I.

The bombing of Coventry was a far more grievous psychological blow to Britain than ever the bombing of London had been. Temporarily, at least, the morale of the citizens of Coventry had been destroyed. "Coventry is dead!" they said and wanted only one thing; to get out of the wrecked city as swiftly as they could.

The temporary demoralization of the citizens of Coventry was no new thing in the bloody history of Britain. In the year 1377, when Britain was at war with France, a powerful French invasion force landed on the Sussex coast, sacked and burned the lovely old town of Rye, and slaughtered many of its townsfolk. The old timbered houses blazed like torches, and the quaint, old cobblestone streets ran red with blood. Such dreadful things were done by the invaders that an old chronicle of the times states, "Rye became a towne of ghostes and dreadfull memories." Such terrible things had happened in the old town, which today is one of Britain's tourist attractions, that the inhabitants left Rye and refused to go back to it until the town fathers threatened to confiscate the property of the townsfolk. After this, five of the town's most prominent members reluctantly went back, to be followed later by the rest of the community.

The new Coventry Cathedral, with shell of old cathedral at left. *Courtesy of the Provost and Chapter of Coventry Cathedral*

111

The citizens of Coventry were made of sterner stuff than the townsfolk of Rye; and after the first feelings of shock and horror had passed, they went back to their ruined city with its badly damaged aircraft and tank factories. Here they worked at the benches and the lathes, standing in the roofless, windowless building, working in the bitter winds and pelting rains until those factories were repaired and working at full speed again. Coventry was not dead, nor was the spirit of its people broken, for within six weeks of that terrible raid the production of aircraft and tanks was back to normal.

After the raid on Coventry, the German propaganda machine coined a new word, *coventrieren*, which means "to coventrate." After 16 more bombing raids on London, the Luftwaffe proceeded to "Coventrate" Southampton, Plymouth, Portsmouth, Devonport, Bristol and Avonmouth, Birmingham, Liverpool and Birkenhead, Sheffield, Manchester, Cardiff, Derby, Swansea, Glasgow and Clyde side, Hull and Tyneside, Belfast, Marrow-in-Furness, and Nottingham.

After London, on which a total of 14,000 tons of high-explosive bombs and 100,000 incendiary bombs were dropped, the most heavily bombed places in Britain were Bristol, Plymouth, Hull, Clydeside, and Merseyside.

Up to the beginning of 1941 there had been little in the way of bombing on the northwest coast of Scotland. To the people who lived here, the London blitz seemed remote, something they felt would not happen to them. This wishful thinking was rudely shattered on the nights of March 13 and 14, 1941, when the burgh of Clydebank near Glasgow was badly blitzed. More than three-quarters of the population of 47,000 were rendered homeless. Under these circumstances, one would imagine that the morale of the Clydesiders could have been damaged, but this was not the case. On the morning after the first raid, a good number of workmen turned up at John Brown's huge shipbuilding yard in spite of the fact that public transport, already inadequate, was further disorganized by the bombing; and numbers of the shipyard employees lived up to 30 miles from their work.

After the savage bombing of Merseyside at the beginning of May, 1941, some ugly and damaging rumors began to circulate. Although without foundation, they were dangerous, the sort of defeatist talk the fifth column and Nazi propagandists thrived on. People were saying that whole trainloads of dead people were being sent from the Merseyside towns for mass cremation; that demented people were marching round the bomb-devastated areas, waving white flags, the token of surrender, and screaming for it all to stop; that food riots were taking place and that martial law had been imposed on these areas.

The situation was ugly enough, without ugly rumors; for, in all, 44,000 Britons died and nearly 51,000 were maimed and seriously wounded before the bombing eased off, owing to the Luftwaffe's being diverted to the Russian front.

The people of Britain's home front had suffered grievously and were to suffer new terror weapons before the war was won, but their sufferings were light compared to the retribution that was to fall on the civilian populations of German towns and cities. The architect of this retribution was ruthless Air Chief Marshal Sir Arthur ("Bomber") Harris, who dedicated himself to the destruction of the towns and cities of the Third Reich. But, in the meantime,

Britain's fate hung in the balance; in the previous summer of 1940, even Winston Churchill had had to face the terrible fact that defeat could happen. He telegraphed President Roosevelt, saying that a time might come when the present Government would lose control and a pro-Nazi government would have to take its place and Britain would be forced to surrender.

7. The War: Air, Sea, and Land

At the beginning of the war, RAF Bomber Command, then under Air Chief Marshal Portal, consisted of 33 operational squadrons. Ten of these were made up of the inadequate Fairey Battle bombers, which had been sent to France to help the ill-fated British Expeditionary Force rescued from Dunkirk and were not truly part of Bomber Command.

There were six squadrons of Blenheim bombers; and these, while too short-range to bomb Germany from England, were forbidden by the French government to operate from French bases before the Nazis occupied France.

Apart from this, there were 17 squadrons made up of Whitley, Wellington, and Hampden bombers, only 209 aircraft in all without even enough trained aircrews to man these adequately.

At the very beginning of the war, the unsuitability and lack of numbers of bombers and trained aircrews, coupled with the noncooperation of the French and the fears of the Chamberlain Government of massive reprisals by the powerful Luftwaffe, prevented the effective bombing of Germany.

Nevertheless, on May 15, 1940, only five days after Winston Churchill became prime minister, 99 aircraft of RAF Bomber Command were sent to attack the oil refineries and railway marshalling yards of the Ruhr. These attacks on Germany were both costly and ineffective, for the combat planes of the Luftwaffe and the well-organized German ground defenses dealt with the British bombers with almost contemptuous ease.

To commence with, the Luftwaffe had highly efficient combat planes, the ME 109 and ME 110, for both day and night operations. These were sent to attack British bombers by means of a most efficient early warning and control scheme. In fact, so effective were the German antiaircraft guns and searchlights that they were capable of dealing with the British bombers without the intervention of the Luftwaffe at all. The German searchlight system worked in close cooperation with the night fighters of the Luftwaffe and made the business of shooting down British bombers easy. By a system of colored searchlights, the German night fighters were directed to intercept the British bombers.

So short was the range of the British bombers at this time that, apart from the Ruhr, which was within striking distance of bombers based in East Anglia, the industrial heart of Germany was a great deal farther from British bombers than the industrial targets of Britain were from German bombers based in occupied France. By day British bombers could see their way to German targets, if they were lucky enough to survive, and a great many did not. By night they were frequently lost, for as yet no adequate instruments were available to guide them to their targets in the dark.

This state of affairs was soon to be remedied, for Britain's scientists described as Back Room Boys and Boffins were working on radio and radar aids known as GEE, H2S, and OBOE, which were to guide British bombers accurately to their targets in the dark.

Up to this early stage of the war, RAF Bomber Command's attacks on Germany had been feeble and sporadic; but the bombing of Mannheim, the first German city to "blitzed" by the British, marked a turning point. The attack had been carried out by 134 bombers on December 13, 1940, and caused considerable dismay in Germany, even though subsequent aerial photographs showed that the damage inflicted was comparatively slight. Thereafter, British bombing raids extended to other German towns and cities, including Berlin, Bremen, Dusseldorf, Hanover, Essen, Cologne, and Hamburg. Radio communiqués concerning these raids became a great morale booster to the British people.

Aircraft workers were already working all-out to build the giant four-engine Handley Page Halifax, Stirling, and Avro Lancaster bombers, which, together with the American B-24 Liberators and B-17 Fortresses, were destined to pound German towns and cities to smoking rubble in the famous "thousand bomber by day—thousand bomber by night" raids yet to come.

In March, 1941, President Roosevelt's Lend-Lease Act was passed, and it gave the president the power to provide Britain with aid that covered everything from finance to food and U.S. weapons and tanks. Winston Churchill described the passage of the Lend-Lease Act as "the most unsordid act in the history of any nation." Nevertheless, this unstinted help from America, which did so much to hearten the British and help them in their struggle, had repercussions. It caused the Nazis to increase their attacks on ships carrying food and war supplies to Britain, and so, inevitably, came the Battle of the Atlantic when the German U-boat "Wolf Packs" and the giant long-range Condor bombers attacked British and Allied convoys with increasing intensity.

Towards the end of 1940, British, Allied, and neutral shipping losses were about 300,000 tons a month. At the beginning of 1941, they had increased to 400,000 tons a month and rose to 700,000 tons by April. Winston Churchill gave orders to the Ministry of Information to cease publishing the figures of the losses, which were having a bad effect on the morale of the British people.

In view of the fact that Britain is a maritime nation, it is odd to think that the British Merchant Service had been, and to some degree still is, considered a "Cinderella service," with many people tending to regard merchant seamen as "misfits" for any other sort of work.

World War II did a great deal to change this attitude, and the humble Merchant Service became the much-glamourized Merchant Navy, with seamen wearing small silver badges in their lapels to prove it. No longer were they "misfits"; they were suddenly national heroes. And heroes they most certainly were, for by the end of World War II, the bitter seas and oceans of the world had claimed the lives of some 50,000 of them.

From the time they left port until they reached their destinations, the ships carrying food and war supplies to beleaguered Britain faced ferocious enemy attack—from the surface, from beneath the surface, and from the air, Nazi battleships and commerce raiders shelled and sank them without mercy, "Wolf Packs" of hunting U-boats torpedoed them, and long-range German bombers deluged them with bombs.

Even when the merchant ships, often slow and poorly armed, were in sight of Britain, there was no respite. Stukas and low-level bombers from bases in occupied France harried them; the long-range guns on the Channel coast blasted at them; and their way to the very dockside itself was strewn with floating mines, magnetic mines, and acoustic mines. It was common to see convoys led by whole fleets of minesweepers, the way to port heralded by the frequent roar of exploding mines. Of all the ships, the most dangerous to serve aboard were the great tankers that carried high-octane gasoline for Britain's fighting aircraft. When hit by shells. bombs. torpedoes, or mines, they erupted into a roaring hell of flame that spread all round the buckling, white-hot ship, making the rescue of the crews impossible.

All too often the whole Thames's mouth from the Kent to the Essex shores was one great sea of leaping flame and smoke from loaded tankers that had struck mines. On one occasion, a tanker was actually being berthed at the Thames Haven oil refinery when it was blown up by a parachute mine that had fallen right alongside the jetty. Even when ships had tied up and were unloading their cargoes, they were not safe from bombing by the Luftwaffe. This happened at the ports of Clydeside, Merseyside, and Bristol, to which merchant ships had been diverted after the enemy bombing attacks on the port of London became intensified.

It was at this grim time, when the arteries of Britain were in danger of being severed, that the British government was faced with manpower problems. The diversion of merchant ships from London and ports on the exposed eastern coast of England to ports on the less exposed western and northwestern coasts required a mass movement of skilled dockers to unload and load the ships. This task demanded considerable tact and careful handling, for dockers are a highly volatile section of the community with their own ways and traditions. Before the war they were classed as "casual workers"; that is to say, they did not work on regular days, but were called upon when needed and then only paid for the ships they loaded or unloaded.

Such a system could obviously not be allowed to continue during the war, and in June, 1940, Ernest Bevin ordered the registration of all dock labor. Later that year, Bevin reorganized the loose structure of dock labor by the appointment of regional port directors, whose task it was to organize and direct dock labor at the ports of the River Clyde and River Mersey where the British merchant ships were now docking.

In March, 1941, and for the first time in Britain's history, British dockers were organized into a permanent work force with a guaranteed minimum wage. This scheme was not only highly successful in achieving a faster turn round of merchant ships, but it also eliminated the social evil of "casual labor." It needed a war to bring a measure of security to one of the hitherto most insecure sections of the British working community.

At this period, too, the first steps were taken to nationalize Britain's railways by integrating the separate railway companies, each with its own working methods and traditions, into a single organization. This was done for greater efficiency and was achieved by the government's providing the British railway companies with a guaranteed annual income of £43 million.

After the dockers and the railways were organized, it was now necessary to reorganize the two ministries that dealt with them. On May 8th 1941, the Ministry of Shipping and the Ministry of Transport became the new Ministry of War Transport.

Britain's harassed government was now faced with an even greater problem than dockers and railways, that of the distribution of manpower. Between the fall of 1940 and the end of 1941, the RAF, the Royal Navy, the army, and the Civil Defence Organisation urgently needed one and three-quarters of a million men and 84,000 thousand women. To meet these requirtments, something like half a million men would have to be taken from the three and a half million already working in war factories. But these factories needed an additional million and a half workers themselves.

There was only one answer to this problem; the women of Britain would have to do as their grandmothers and mothers had done during World War I: Work at the factory benches. A million and a half women were needed, and, to complicate matters, a large number of skilled men would be needed to train this great army of women in many new and exacting tasks.

It was now vital to weld Britain's war industry into a coherent form, and to achieve this, two things were done. A scheme of "protected establishments" was organized that would ensure that workers in factories and establishments vital to war production would remain where they were working. The second requirement was that the government should have the power to register workers and direct them into industries essential to the war.

So it was that in March, 1940, the Registration of Employment Order came into being, and men over 41 and women between 20 and 21 were the first to register. The registration for women was later extended, so that all women between the ages of 18 and 50 were required by law to register.

Under the Registration of Employment Order, men and women who had registered but who were not employed in essential war work were interviewed at employment exchanges and asked if they would be prepared to undertake essential war work for which they might be suitable. It was very much the case of the steel fist in the velvet glove; one could go willingly or receive a compulsory direction and be sent. Most people went willingly. Something like a million people received direction orders under the act, most of them in the building and engineering trades.

To tighten the government's grip on war industry even more, the Essential Works Order was passed on March 5, 1941. This gave Ernest Bevin enormous and unprecedented powers, for he could declare any form of work done in any kind of factory essential to the war effort if necessary. Moreover, no management could dismiss any employee nor could any employee leave his place of work without the permission of a national-service officer from the Ministry of Labor.

Few realized it at the time, but the Essential Works Order was a blessing in disguise to the workers of Britain. Ernest Bevin had been a worker and a dedicated trade unionist himself, and no man knew the working classes of Britain better than he did. He knew that to make the Essential Works Order viable and thus ensure massive war production output, the six million workers of all categories for whom he was responsible would have to be kept happy and content in their tasks. Thus he began reforms for better wages and better working conditions.

Among those who benefited under Bevin's administration were the hard-pressed and hitherto underpaid and underprivileged men of Britain's all-important Merchant Navy, in which able-bodied seamen of years' experience had received a beggarly £8 per month up to and including the outbreak of the war. Now they had to stay put in their ships, whereas in peacetime they could choose to work in any ship they liked. However, they now received far better wages plus additional danger money, and their pay was guaranteed while they were ashore, which had not been their lot in peacetime. They also received longer periods of well-deserved shore leave.

The forthright and capable "Ernie" Bevin, noted for his vast contempt for "intellectuals," had his own ideas about the army too. He did not consider that every man called up for military service would necessarily be doing essential work. He knew that many soldiers were still doing nonessential and sometimes even ridiculous tasks of peacetime. There was the classic example of a Bachelor of Science, who had been drafted into the army and was found in the cookhouse helping to peel a mountain of potatoes.

"Ernie" Bevin exerted a great deal of pressure on these matters. In the end, Winston Churchill issued an order that stated categorically that the demands of the armed forces would be looked into very carefully. There was a general tightening up of the armed forces all round. The girls and women in the Women's Auxiliary Air Force (WAAF) and the Women's Royal Naval Service (WRNS —called Wrens) and the Women's Royal Army Corps (WRAC) were subject to service discipline, although in a modified form—the first time such a thing had happened to women in the history of Britain.

Not only was there a tightening up in the armed forces, but also in the Civil Defence organizations. The Auxiliary Fire Service, the Police War Reserve, and the newly created Civil Defence Reserve now became incorporated into the Civil Defence Forces, which men could be compelled to join if necessary.

While the government was grappling with manpower problems, all was far from well with Britain's war economy. The 1941 wartime budget introduced by Sir Kingsley Wood gave the nation a nasty shock, especially the working classes. To prevent inflation, the government needed £500 million; and to obtain this, the standard rate of income tax went up to ten shillings in the pound. The income tax exemption rate was also lowered, so that millions of people who were in the lower income groups, which had previously been exempt from income tax, now had to pay.

It was at this period that postwar credits came into existence, a system whereby some of the money taken in taxation would be repaid when the taxpayer had reached the retirement age of 65 after the war. Later, this age limit was reduced to 60, but there was little satisfaction to the taxpayer. For although the government paid interest on the postwar credits, their value had diminished considerably by the time they were paid out.

Many people were critical of the government's handling of the nation's finances. Some wanted a wage freeze imposed, whereas others wanted to see a set wage for all civilians, irrespective of what work they might be doing.

Ernest Bevin rejected all this, declaring that the peacetime system of collective bargaining between management and trade unions would have to remain. He said that the wages of the lowest paid workers were so low that they could not be frozen. If they were frozen, it would be necessary to raise the wages of millions of low paid workers to give them parity with other workers. If this were done, whole industries would have to be subsidized by the government to meet the cost of raising these low wages.

In the meantime, the government had to deal with the ever rising cost of living, considerably aggravated by increasing black market operations and profiteering. It was a simple business to fix the prices of rationed food and consumer goods, such as there were; but without rationing, the food and the goods just vanished or went "under the counter." This meant that the wealthy could buy unrationed food and goods in bulk while the less fortunate got nothing.

Such nonrationed foods as poultry, rabbits, tomatoes, and onions, for example, all plentiful in peacetime, just vanished from public sale. While some food items seemed to disappear, there was an embarrassing plentitude of carrots, a bewildering circumstance the Ministry of Food joyfully exploited. Everywhere notices appeared exhorting the public to eat carrots. Carrots were good for you; carrots even helped you to see better in the dark and thus enabled you to walk fearlessly in the blackout. Children's toffee apples, apples coated with a thin layer of sticky toffee and impaled on a short stick, were replaced by "Toffee carrots."

Such blatant hucksterism did not help the British public much, for the lists of food shortages, the lengths of the food queues, and the patient faces of the queuers grew longer and longer while many uncontrolled but expensive foods and goods were still available to the wealthy.

8. Austerity Measures

By the summer of 1941, Britain was again faced with manpower problems and again the Ministry of Labour was constrained to survey the nation's manpower resources for a solution. The survey established that an additional two million men and women were needed for the armed forces and the industrial front. Of this two million, half a million extra aircraft workers would be needed for the building of new-type bombers of greater range, greater bomb capacity, and heavier protective armaments. In the meantime, such was the urgent demand for fighting men that it was becoming necessary to release physically fit men from the Civil Defence to be drafted into the armed forces.

After assessing the situation, Ministers Bevin and Anderson decreed that all Britons between the ages of 18 and 60, regardless of sex, would be required to perform national service in one form or another. So it was that Britain was forced by the pressures of a war of survival to take a step which dismayed the entire nation and its leaders:

Women workers in Plessey's wartime factory. *Courtesy of London Transport Board*

to conscript women into national service. The conscription of women was unprecedented, and, to begin with, Winston Churchill rejected the whole idea. Even Ernest Bevin, used to dealing with difficult labor problems, was reluctant to use his powers to conscript women and did all he could to persuade them to *volunteer* for service. Yet even his considerable persuasive powers were not sufficient for this, and at the beginning of December, 1941, the British public was shocked and dismayed to hear that women were to be conscripted.

As might be expected, the women of Britain were outraged at this infringement of their ancient liberties, especially those in such genteel occupations as secretaries and typists. The thought of wearing overalls and working at benches in noisy factories or of being drafted into the Women's Forces of the Crown, where they would have to mix with "rough types," frankly terrified them.

What they did not realize then was that they were taking a very long stride towards women's liberation and that the "rough types" they would have to mix with would not only immeasurably extend their outlook on life, but also give them a satisfying comradeship they had never known existed, to say nothing of extending their vocabulary.

Their fears, however, were not to be wondered at, for they imagined that, like the Russian women, they would be conscripted into the armed forces to fight alongside the men. Their relief was great when they found that after having been drafted into the armed forces, supplied with uniforms, and given token drills, most of them continued to do the same sort of office and domestic work that they had done in peacetime, although some of them did work alongside the gunners of the antiaircraft batteries.

With the vast majority of Britain's women now working at full-time jobs, the married men had to look after themselves; and although they complained about it, it increased their ability to look after themselves on the domestic front. In addition to this, the men found that a great deal more could be done with two salaries than one, although they deplored the increasingly independent attitude of their womenfolk, numbers of whom earned much more than their husbands.

Most of the male public regarded the conscription of their women as a personal affront, at least until they got used to it. On the other hand, there was one section of the male community, who though suspicious at first, came to regard the matter with satisfaction, if not pleasure. These were the agricultural workers, especially those in the remoter country places of Britain; for the sudden influx of buxom young women of the Women's Land Army, clad in tight, brown riding breeches, well-filled green jumpers, and wide-brimmed stetson-type hats brought life and glamour to many a sleepy village, renewed hope for many a lonely bachelor and, sad to say, to many who were not bachelors.

The fact that many of the girls of the Women's Land Army did not know a cow from a bull, a sheep from a ram, a sow from a boar, or a gelding from a stallion did not matter in the least. The farmers and farmhands went to great pains to instruct them, and the girls, especially the more gently nurtured ones, learned the facts of life in a way their parents would not have been able to teach them. Nevertheless, great numbers of these girls grew to enjoy the open-air life and stayed in the country to marry.

In a world very short of transport, one of the first things the Land Army girls learned was how to "thumb a ride" and hitchhike from village to village. It was a habit that caught on and became general with wayfarers.

The girls of the Women's Land Army, some 80,000 of them—at an official minimum wage of £2 8s. a week, which, if their employer was mean, they sometimes did not get—performed a variety of agricultural tasks. Some grew fruit and vegetables; others became official ratcatchers. They learned how to milk cows, herd and shear sheep, clean out cattle pens, make hay, keep poultry, cut and thresh grain crops, pull sugar beets on icy cold mornings, hoe row upon row of turnips, and, in time, give as good as they got from the country lads they worked with.

Six thousand Amazons of the Women's Land Army

belonged to the "Timber Corps," which cut down trees and worked in saw mills. Others learned to handle horse plows and tractors. A seemingly fragile girl, who had once worked in a ladies' hairdressing salon, beat all comers in a plowing match in Yorkshire.

Generally speaking, life in the Women's Land Army was pleasant enough for country-bred women and the more robust types of girls. But for town and city-bred girls, it could be something of an ordeal, and much depended on the type of farmer they worked for.

British farms are among the most modern in the world, and farmers and their families are good and kindly people generally, but there are exceptions. In isolated instances, even to this day, some British farms are so primitive that they almost border on the neolithic. Water has to be pumped or fetched from wells, and indoor bathing and toilet facilities are nonexistent.

The lot of a land army girl who worked on such a farm was not a happy one. Her hours were from dawn to dusk seven days a week; and her only privacy, a small, spartan bedroom. There were no cinemas or dance halls for miles, and her annual leave was a miserly seven days. In addition to all this, the farmer's wife might regard her as a rival for her husband's affections, which made matters worse all round.

If a land army girl was unhappy or dissatisfied for any reason, she could appeal to the Women's Land Army representative. This did not always prove satisfactory, for the representatives were often farmers' wives themselves and were therefore biased. The only other resort for the land army girl was to leave her job and go home, and in doing this, she risked imprisonment. It must be said, however, that no land army girl ever was imprisoned, owing largely to the fact that imprisonment did not help the war effort.

By this time Britain had settled down into the gray New Order of Austerity. Food, while not scarce, generally speaking, was strictly limited in variety. Potatoes, which were not rationed, dominated the culinary scene. What the British housewives learned to do with the humble spud was quite astonishing. In addition to serving it baked, boiled, and fried (when fat was available), they made potato pies filled with leftovers, potato cakes, and potato scones, flavored with a few shreds of cheese and surprisingly tasty.

The more ambitious wives, and indeed their husbands, made potato and other vegetable wines. Though these brews sometimes tasted awful, their undeniable potency brought a great deal more good cheer than the limited quantities of watery wartime beer, which was supplemented on rare occasions by Scotch whiskey and other liquor.

Bread, like potatoes, was not rationed, but the white bread of peacetime was no more, one of the reasons for this being that the flour mills and bakeries of Britain had been badly hit by German bombing. Then the Ministry of Food introduced the abhorred "national wheatmeal loaf," a name that was misleading, to say the least, for it was composed of "flour" from which 85 percent of the wheat had been extracted. In spite of the efforts of the Ministry of Food to popularize this gray, soggy, indigestible honor, the British public loathed it and threw it in the trash bins, to the birds, and to the pigs, who sniffed it reluctantly. It was, the public felt, not only unfit to eat, but also responsible for skin complaints, indigestion, and a host of other stomach ailments.

The government tried to discourage this rejection of the national wheatmeal loaf by imposing small fines on those who threw it out. It made no difference, for the national wheatmeal loaf was despised by the British public, who either made their own bread when they could or filled up on other things such as biscuits when they could get these. Biscuits could certainly be found in the shops, but like most other food items in Britain, they had been reduced in quality and variety. In prewar days there were over 400 varieties of biscuits in Britain; now there were only 200.

But it was the rationing of tea that probably hit the British people hardest. Tea drinking in Britain is not merely a national habit; it is a national institution. Some foreigners even think it is a vice. Farmhands sit under hedges and drink tea. The men of the gangs repairing roads sit on their piles of earth drinking tea. "Spider men" drink tea on the lofty steel girders of tall buildings under construction. Men repairing gas mains, water mains, and electrical mains beneath the surface of the earth have mugs of tea beside them in their holes and trenches.

Thus, the British people hoarded their four-ounce-per-week tea ration as if it were gold, brewed the same tea twice if they had to, and reluctantly heeded the government's exhortation not to have "one for the pot"; that is to say, put an extra teaspoonful of tea in the teapot to ensure a good strong brew. They heeded, but in heeding felt that they were relinquishing an ancient privilege.

The old and sacred institutions of British soccer, rugby football, cricket, tennis, and horse racing were hard hit too at this gray period. Soccer clubs no longer existed, for their players had been drafted into the armed forces or into war production. Arsenal, one of Britain's most famous professional soccer teams, had lost all of its players except two, and its famous stadium at Highbury, London, became a massive concrete civil defense headquarters. The world-famous Rugby football ground at Twickenham had been dug up to grow vegetables. The Home Guard drilled on Wimbledon tennis courts. Kennington Oval, Surrey, the home of British cricket, became a prisoner-of-war camp, and exclusive Epsom racecourse in Surrey had been requisitioned by the military.

In 1942, Minister Hugh Dalton of the Board of Trade brought in his "austerity regulations," which, among other things, were designed to save textiles. They achieved this, but made British civilian clothing drab to the extreme.

Women's clothing was now without embroidery and with the number of pleats, seams, and buttonholes of each garment strictly limited. Cuffs on men's trousers were prohibited as were double cuffs on jackets. Shirts, boots and shoes, socks and hats were also subjected to the austerity regulations.

At this same time, the British people had to endure another ordeal of fire, destruction, and death from the air. These became known as the Baedeker Raids, because the towns and cities attacked by the Luftwaffe were classified as tourist attractions in the Baedeker guidebooks. Air Chief Marshal Sir Arthur ("Bomber") Harris, chief of RAF Bomber Command in 1942, has been unjustly blamed for these raids, which were aimed at some of Britain's most beautiful and historic cities.

In the spring of 1942, the chiefs of RAF Bomber Command wished to compare the effect of saturation by incendiary bombs to that of saturation by high-explosive bombs. It was Sir Arthur Harris who ordered the fire raids on the Baltic towns of Lubeck and Rostock in March and April of 1942.

Lubeck, with its ancient timbered houses, was an ideal target for such an experimental operation, for, in the words of Sir Arthur Harris, Lubeck was "built more like a fire-lighter than a human habitation." The quaint old German town went up in flames like a funeral pyre in a deadly hail of incendiary bombs from the big, four-engine Lancaster bombers, which were used for the first time. Lubeck, like Coventry, was gutted, and 312 people died in the raid.

The Nazis, furious at the fire bombardment of Lubeck and Rostock and ignoring the fact that they had previously dealt with Coventry in like manner, retaliated savagely.

On April 24, 1942, the ancient and beautiful city of Exeter in the county of Devonshire was raided by 25 enemy bombers, which ravaged the city with fire bombs and extra heavy high-explosive bombs. The ancient town of Bath in the county of Somerset, once a Roman spa, received the same treatment, and 400 of its townsfolk died.

The old and lovely city of Norwich in the county of Norfolk was heavily raided three nights in succession. The city of York was bombed, and its ancient and famous guild-hall was destroyed. On May 3, 1942, the city of Exeter was attacked by 90 bombers, the cathedral was damaged, and many ancient churches and buildings were destroyed completely.

On May 31, June 2, and June 6, the city of Canterbury, Kent, was bombed; and although the world-famous cathedral was only slightly damaged, part of the residential area of the city was demolished. However, in spite of heavy damage to property in these three raids, casualties were light, for only 100 people were killed.

Towards the end of June, 1942, the city of Norwich was again attacked, and this was the last of the notorious Baedeker Raids.

In the meantime, RAF Bomber Command had retaliated savagely in this monstrous game of tit for tat. Retaliation came like a thunderclap on May 30, 1942, in the first "thousand bomber" raid of the war. For two and a half hours, British bombers thundered over Cologne, whose cathedral made a prominent aiming point, in a new formation called the bomber stream. For every minute of that two and a half hours, seven British bombers dropped their deadly loads on Cologne, completely devastating 600 acres of the city and killing thousands of its inhabitants.

This raid marked the beginning of the period that culminated in the combined British-American air offensive, the legendary "thousand American bombers by day and thousand British bombers by night."

But the Americans had yet to come to Britain. . . .

9. American Aid and Increased British Effort

WITH THE BOMBING of Pearl Harbor by the Japanese on Sunday, December 7, 1941, the United States entered the war against the Axis powers. The Japanese army advanced swiftly against the American-held Philippine Islands and against British-held Hong Kong, Malaya, and Burma. Britain immediately declared war on Japan, while Germany and Italy declared war on the United States in support of Japan.

Britain no longer stood alone, but had the armed might and vast resources of America at her side.

The first contingent of 3,000 American soldiers landed at Belfast on January 26, 1942, and more American troops poured into the ports of Scotland, into the port of London, and many other ports on England's southern coast.

The British public was both impressed and disconcerted at the coming of the GIs. For one thing, the GIs appeared to be more smartly uniformed than the British Tommies and received a great deal more pay. This caused considerable jealousy at first, which was not helped by the differences in character of the Americans and the British.

Many Britons were deeply disappointed to discover that the majority of their new allies had no home ties with Britain. Even though they spoke an odd sort of English, they seemed more like foreigners, and many of them had foreign names as well.

The younger Britons were not in the least dismayed about this; rather were they intrigued to find that the new-comers in many cases spoke like the gangsters they had seen in films. Admiring this potent form of speech, the younger Britons began to copy it.

The Americans were shocked by the small rations of the British and were hurt and angry when their offers of food and other luxuries were rejected coldly. As yet the Americans did not comprehend the pride inherent in even the poorest classes of the British community.

The vast amount of transport the Americans brought with them was an equal source of wonder to the British. Gasoline was unlimited, and everybody seemed to have some sort of motorized transport, ranging from motorcycles to jeeps. Then there were fleets of officers' staff cars, trucks, tracked and half-tracked vehicles, massive bulldozers, and mechanical shovels.

Even more interesting were the unlimited supplies of luxuries the Americans had; cigarettes, tobacco, candy and chewing gum, razor blades and scented soap, coffee—as rare in Britain as snow in the Sahara Desert—and, above all, the sheer silk stockings that sent luxury-starved British women into raptures.

The one thing that angered British civilians and fighting men alike was the well-paid, smartly uniformed Americans walking into British bars and drinking up the small supplies of beer and liquor, and sometimes walking out with the Britons' girl friends. These circumstances frequently caused brawls until a mutual understanding and tolerance were achieved.

One of the greatest barriers between the Americans and their British hosts to begin with was the flamboyance and natural generosity of the former and the inherent reticence and pride of the latter. At first, the Americans said that the Limeys were offhand and unfriendly, and the Britons said that the Yanks were too bigheaded and full of bull. In time, however, the inherent good nature of the Americans and the inherent tolerance of the Britons bridged the gap.

At this early period also a number of ugly brawls between white and colored Americans occurred. This puzzled the British, who at this time had no color problem of their own. Equally bewildering to the British public was the bad feeling that sometimes was manifest between the Americans and some of the British Commonwealth troops. In particular, friction between the Americans and the French Canadians resulted in a number of ugly scenes.

There were, however, some Americans who had close and strong ties with Britain, and these came to love the old country deeply. They plunged happily into every conceivable form of British social life, including sport, learning the arts of cricket and soccer and teaching their hosts the mysteries of American football and baseball.

Some of these young Americans learned to cherish the ancient heritage of Britain as much as, and in some cases even more than, the British themselves. They formed groups to help with the upkeep of ancient British churches, and along the bleak and dangerous eastern shores of England, American personnel from several U.S. Army airfields even helped with the manning and launching of the life-boats of the various towns and villages.

These ties were further strengthened by marriage, for after the war something like 80,000 British girls who had married Americans returned to the United States with their husbands. And some of the Americans remained to live in Britain.

It did not take long for the Americans to settle down, and by July, 1943, the American services network was broadcasting programs of lively music and American comedy that were appreciated by great numbers of Britons, especially those in the younger age groups.

While the Americans were settling down to their training, building their airfields and mustering their fleets of combat planes and bombers, Britain's war industry was gathering more and more momentum. Everybody was working at full capacity, and many Britons were even doing two jobs.

At this period, thousands of volunteer workers from all walks of life, even from the House of Commons, were helping to increase the steadily growing output of munitions of war.

Men who worked fewer than 60 hours a week and women who worked fewer than 55 hours were compelled by law to do fire watching one night a week. On this cold and dreary vigil, the watchers, muffled in greatcoats and wearing helmets of heat-resistant plastic, perched on the tops of tall buildings to watch during air raids for fires started by enemy incendiary bombs.

Before the war, Britain had been in the grip of mass unemployment, but now there was more than enough work for everyone. The coming of the Americans had provided work for an additional half million people. The heavy industries—steel and iron production, shipbuilding, engineering, chemical and explosive industries, and oil refining—now employed five million workers, two million more than in times of peace.

There was a massive increase in aircraft production, for soon British and American bombers would strike devastating blows at the very heart of the Third Reich. At the beginning of the war, there had been 19 major British aircraft companies operating 45 factories. By 1943 these same companies were operating 323 factories. The workers of these factories were the most highly paid of Britain's war workers—and they earned their pay. Aircraft production in Britain rose from 8,000 planes in 1939 to 26,461 in 1944, with a total of 120,000 produced over the entire period of the war. One of the most successful aircraft ever produced in Britain during the war was the unorthodox Mosquito. This versatile, fast, highly maneuverable plane was built entirely of plywood, was twin-engined, and proved of inestimable worth both as a fast bomber and as a highly effective night fighter.

While the aircraft factories were churning out an ever-increasing number of warplanes, the automobile manufacturers of Britain were turning out engines for both warplanes and tanks. The famous Rolls Royce Company and the Ford Motor Company combined their expertise to produce engines for combat planes and bombers, and from this union of two great companies emerged the incomparable Rolls Royce Merlin engine.

The mighty Imperial Chemical Industries (ICI), which had 25 vast factories working at full production by the end of the war, was producing every conceivable type of chemical necessary for explosives and other war materials. Forty-three Royal Ordnance factories, employing 300,000 workers of both sexes, were producing an ever increasing volume of arms, ammunition, shells, bombs, explosives, heavy artillery, mines, and tanks in the greatest war industry complex the world had ever seen. Largest of these Royal Ordnance factories was the one at Chorley in Lancashire, which specialized in explosive filling. This huge complex, which employed something like 35,000 workers, had 1,500 separate buildings covering 1,000 acres.

The ordnance factories were supplemented by peacetime factories that had been reorganized and retooled for war production. For instance, a onetime chocolate factory now filled antiaircraft rockets with propellants and high explosive.

In time, so great did the output of war munitions become that there was no room in the factories for the storing of shells, which had to be stockpiled in great dumps by the roadsides.

However, there were drones even in Britain's now roaring hive of war industry. The number of deserters from the armed forces fluctuated between 20,000 and 80,000. As it was almost impossible for deserters to obtain such essential wartime documents as ration and identity cards, the majority of the deserters either took to crime to live or joined the ranks of the black marketeers.

The black market was undoubtedly a major menace in Britain during the war, for it was increasingly well organized. Food that should have reached the public at a fair price was purchased illegally in bulk in the warehouses and then sold at an exorbitant profit.

The black market in clothing flourished partly because those who lost their books of clothing ration coupons could get them replaced with little or no investigation as to how they were lost. At the beginning of the war, nearly a million people claimed to have lost their clothing ration books; and, as a result, something like 27 million extra coupons were issued. It was a profitable business to "lose" an easily replaceable clothing ration book when it would fetch £5 in the black market.

The black market also flourished in Ireland, where fat cattle, pigs, poultry, eggs, cheese, and butter could easily be smuggled into Northern Ireland and thence to Scotland, Wales, and England.

The government tried to control these illegal activities with a "secret squad" from the Ministry of Food, whose duty it was to arrest black marketeers, who could be fined up to £500 and jailed for two years. These government snoopers, as the public called them, were not too popular in Britain, for their methods of operation were, by necessity, often devious. For example, "snoopers" would visit clothes shops and, posing as ordinary customers, try to buy clothing with loose coupons. This was illegal. If the storekeeper was foolish enough to comply, then he was arrested on the spot.

A gang of skilled forgers made certificates that enabled them to buy food and other rationed materials in the guise of wholesalers. As a result, several million pounds' worth of goods was channeled into the black market.

There were other forms of crime in wartime Britain. Something like 187,000 people were successfully prosecuted through the war for offenses against the defense regulations. These were mostly for offending against the blackout regulations. In view of the existence of the blackout, it is surprising to find that crimes of violence against individuals increased very little. Motoring offenses naturally decreased, owing to gasoline rationing, and in 1943 there were only 100,000 successful prosecutions as compared to 360,000 in the first year of the war when gasoline was easier to obtain. That same year 30,000 people were successfully prosecuted for offenses against the regulations controlling industry, with 12,500 found guilty of offenses against the Control of Employment Order.

As the war went on, boys and girls were mobilized to help the war effort. Already, youngsters in the Boy Scout and Girl Guide organizations had proved their worth as messengers and general helpers during the blitz. And the Air Ministry had formed a uniformed Air Training Corps, which was immediately successful in its appeal, for it soon had some 200,000 eager boys in its ranks.

Every youngster in Britain was now being encouraged in some activity that would contribute towards the war effort. In addition to their normal lessons at school, boys were encouraged to learn pig, rabbit, and poultry breeding and to "dig for victory" to contribute vegetables to the nation's food stocks. Girls were taught how to "make-do-and-mend" with food and clothing.

At harvest time thousands of excited boys and girls went to specially organized harvest camps all over the country and helped to gather in the crops. Most notable of all was the vast amount of salvage materials the boys and girls collected for the war effort. In response to Lord Beaverbrook's appeal, they collected great numbers of old aluminum pots and pans, which would help to build Spitfire combat planes.

The enthusiastic children scoured scrap heaps and dumps, corporation rubbish tips, and trash cans for every conceivable kind of salvage material that might be of some use to the war effort and then took their finds to the special salvage depots that were organized to receive them.

Where kitchen waste was available, it was collected for pig food. Wastepaper was collected and tied up in bundles; barrow loads of old cans, bottles, bones, rags, and jam jars were wheeled in handcarts, carried in sacks, or driven in trucks to the salvage depots all over Britain to be converted into anything that might help win the war.

British children watched with a pleasure not shared by their elders when men with oxyacetylene torches cut down the iron railings that surrounded schools, churches, homes, parks, public buildings, and even cemeteries, and then helped the men load the iron into trucks. The children knew that this old iron would be magically converted into bombs and shells and tanks and guns to defeat the twentieth-century bogeyman, Adolf.

10. Wartime Entertainment in Britain and Harsher Food Rationing

At the beginning of the war, all places of mass entertainment, such as sports stadia, racetracks, motion-picture theaters, dance halls, and theaters, were closed to lessen the risk of high casualties during bombing raids. However, it was not long before dance halls, motion-picture theaters, and theaters were open again, although they had to close by 10:00 p.m. Football, too, was permitted, although with limited numbers of spectators.

The greatest mass entertainment for the British people at this time was provided by the British Broadcasting Corporation. At the outbreak of the war, the BBC had shut down its Regional Services and in their place opened the Home Service, which stayed on the air whatever happened. This was achieved by grouped transmitters, suitably masked to prevent their detection by the enemy. If one transmitter was bombed or had to shut down for any reason, the broadcasting continued almost without break from another station. And everybody went to enormous trouble and inconvenience to ensure that broadcasting continued. Performers and technicians alike slept in the transmitting stations to make sure that they were there when needed. The concert hall in Broadcasting House, London, was converted into a huge dormitory with beds on the floor, where people by hundreds slept, with curtains to separate the sexes.

On one occasion, the author, who had been asked to broadcast in the series "In Town Tonight" in connection with his experiences at sea, was unable to get home because of heavy bombing. He and his wife spent the night in a small studio in Broadcasting House, sleeping quite comfortably on camp beds and only suffering from lack of fresh air.

It was at this time that a clever little comedian from Liverpool, a place notable for the high quality of its entertainers, began to be heard on the air. His name was Tommy Handley, and he and his team of comics provided an endless stream of sharp wit and humor that did so much to turn Britons' thoughts from the grimness of war that at length Tommy and his team became a public institution.

Tommy was the leader of the BBC's comedy series "It's That Man Again" (ITMA for short), a clever, quick-witted and humorous satire directed at everybody: the enemy, the British public, the war in general. In the role of Minister of Aggravation, Tommy sniped endlessly at British bureaucracy and Nazi nastiness.

His technique was to set himself up in the various positions of Britain's traditionally pompous figures and then proceed to demolish them with a barrage of clever and humorous nonsense. As His Washout the Mayor of the fictitious coastal resort of Foaming-at-the-Mouth, Tommy sniped skillfully and uproariously at the pride and pomposity of public office. As Squire of the Manor of Much Fiddling, he presented a zany image of Britain's traditional country squires.

He poured a torrent of satire on the managers of war factories and diminished the stature of the enemy with his German spy character Funf, whose only lines in outrageously Teutonic English over an imaginary telephone were "Dis is Funf speakink" and "Funf has spoken."

Eventually, Tommy Handley surrounded himself with a host of zany characters whose catchphrases became part of wartime Britain. There was the Diver, whose lines consisted mainly of "Don't forget the diver, gents. Don't forget the diver" and "I'm going down now" amid the bursting of sound-effects bubbles. The latter phrase was an immediate success with the bomber pilots and fighter pilots of the RAF, who shouted gleefully into their radio, "I'm going down now!" when they swept down on German targets to drop their bombs and when they hurtled in to attack enemy combat planes.

There was Mrs. Mopp, the corporation cleaner, who personified the great army of Britain's cleaning ladies and whose catchphrase in suggestive tones was, "Can I do you now, sir?"

There was Señor So-So, His Tomship's Secretary, whose mangled brand of English had to be heard to be believed. There was perpetually inebriated Colonel Chinstrap, whose utterance, "I don't mind if I do" can still be heard in British bars by those accepting drinks from others.

Rivalling ITMA in popularity was "Bighearted" Arthur Askey's show, "Band Wagon." Comedian Arthur Askey, as physically active and nimble-witted as ever, still entertains on British television and radio shows.

As well-beloved as Tommy Handley and Arthur Askey was Miss Vera Lynn, whose songs, especially "We'll Meet Again" and "The White Cliffs of Dover," still tug at the heartstrings. Miss Lynn did a great deal more than sing hauntingly nostalgic songs. She visited the sick and injured in hospitals and in her series "Sincerely Yours," broadcast on the Forces Program, she heartened Britain's fighting men all over the world with news of their families and loved ones, so that at last she became known as "the Sweetheart of the Forces." Another great favorite among Britain's wartime entertainers was Cyril Fletcher, with his hilarious and endless stream of "Odd Odes," while Vic Oliver, Ben Lyon, and Bebe Daniels had their own radio show, "Hi, Gang."

As the war went on, the factories and military camps all over Britain had their own radio shows on the air. There was "Ack-Ack-Beer-Beer," which utilized the not inconsiderable amount of talent to be found in the ranks of the men and women of the army who manned the antiaircraft gun sites and barrage balloon sites.

The war factories had their own radio program, "Works Wonders," in which talented workers entertained their fellow workers during the lunch period.

The Women's Auxiliary Air Force (WAAFS) also had its own radio show called "Women in Wartime."

For the more academically minded, there was the

BBC's "Brains Trust," devised by Producer Howard Thoms. It derived its name from the terms by which President Roosevelt described his advisers. To begin with, the "Brains Trust" show consisted of Question Master Donald Mc-Cullough and a team of three wise men: Dr. Julian Huxley, who had the ability to bring science down to the level of the man in the street, Professor Cyril Joad, and Commander A. B. Campbell, R.N., Retired. The show was a contest of wits between these three sages, who had to try to answer, not always with success, an infinite variety of questions sent in by the public. The "Brains Trust," which eventually had something like 12 million listeners, included in its erudite ranks such famous men as Dr. Malcolm Sargent, the famous orchestra conductor; Sir William Beveridge, who devised the Beveridge Report; and Colonel Walter Elliot.

In spite of the risks of bombing, something like 30 million people were moviegoers who saw mostly American films. Because the military call-up had drastically affected the British film industry, six out of every seven films shown in Britain at this time came from America.

The favorite film of the wartime British public was David Selznick's spectacular *Gone with the Wind,* released in 1942. The British loved this film then, and they still love it 30 years later, for it is still shown in British motion-picture theaters.

As the war continued, the British film industry began to revive under the influence of a newcomer to the film world. He was a wealthy flour miller named J. Arthur Rank, who was later knighted. He formed the Rank Film Organisation, which produced a number of notable war documentary films with the help of such producers as the

Boulting brothers, David Lean, Michael Balcon, and others. During this period many British film stars emerged, including John Mills, Margaret Lockwood, Stewart Granger, James Mason, and Rex Harrison.

Such was the spate of war documentaries that eventually the British public became heartily sick of them and welcomed the latest American films, especially the lush musicals. One notable film also of this period was *The Great Dictator*, in which Charles Chaplin reduced Adolf Hitler to an hilarious figure of nonsense.

In spite of the dangers of bombing (60 motion-picture theaters were destroyed before the war ended) and the entertainments tax, which made seats increasingly expensive, London movie houses continued to operate. Between 25 and 30 million adults and children visited them each week. The 20 Grenada movie houses, in fact, made history, for apart from one that was demolished by bombing and nine others that had to close for varying periods, the remaining ten remained open continuously and never stopped a show, even when the blitz was at its worst. Grenada, in fact, contributed much to the war effort in their own fashion. They offered all-night entertainment and shelter to those who could enjoy five feature films in one night, interspersed with community singing and amateur "turns" by members of the audience. Many people even took their bedding to movie houses, which thus became wartime community centers.

Britain's fighting men, factory workers, and allies were also entertained by the Entertainments National Service Association, ENSA, directed by the famous theatrical producer Basil Dean. The function of ENSA was to provide entertainment for troops in remote and isolated parts of the world, and hosts of famous British and American film stars, singers, and musicians appeared in ENSA concerts.

In 1940 the government, with a grant of £25,000, launched an organization called the Council for Education in Music and the Arts, CEMA, the function of which was to ensure that music and the arts did not languish during wartime. CEMA sponsored painting exhibitions in provincial towns and, in addition, engaged the elite Old Vic Company, headed by Dame Sybil Thorndyke, to entertain the miners of South Wales. The Sadler's Wells Ballet Company also toured Britain's industrial towns.

Notable actors and artists like Sir Laurence Olivier, Yehudi Menuhin, and others provided free concerts all over Britain in spite of the bombing and almost insurmountable transport and other difficulties. From the beginning of the war, Dame Myra Hess organized concerts in the National Gallery, denuded of its priceless paintings, which had been carefully stored for safekeeping. The concerts, which took place in a basement, were not without incident. An unexploded bomb blew up in the gallery during a performance, and it is on record that the audience did not move and the performers continued playing Beethoven's Rasoumovsky Quartet without faltering.

For those who preferred spectator sports, the armed forces provided soccer and rugby football matches, and by 1943 these sports had revived to almost peacetime proportions. At international matches as many as 60,000 spectators could be heard roaring their approval or disapproval with peacetime gusto. To make the scene even more interesting, the American troops in Britain introduced the British public to baseball, relaying the mysteries and intricacies of this intriguing new game over a system of loudspeakers. The age-old sacred institution of cricket was also revived with matches played between the British home forces and teams selected from the troops of the British Commonwealth stationed in Britain.

But while British entertainment and sport were increasing, food rationing continued on a widening scale. By 1943 food rationing had become part of the British way of life, and Britons were eating things they had never seen before. Like their remote Scandinavian ancestors, they ate whalemeat, with fried onions, when they could get onions, to disguise the oily, fishy flavor. A few stouthearted souls even tried eating shark meat, but rejected it with disgust for its latrinelike odor and even worse flavor.

Strange fowl were appearing on the menu now, and the Scots people who lived near the coast returned to the ways of their ancestors, eating a variety of seabirds, which they first skinned and then steeped in brine to remove the fishy flavor. An aged East Anglian, who supplemented his old-age pension by shooting wild fowl in the marshes of Suffolk, regularly sent his London relations large, messy parcels of skinned coot, which they called "substitute chicken." And *substitute* this unusual addition to the war-time menu most certainly was, for the flesh of the fowl was almost as black as its feathers.

Youngsters who lived near sea cliffs risked life and limb to collect baskets of seabirds' eggs, for which there was always a market since the majority of the public could not expect to get more than 30 fresh eggs per person per year. The rest of the time they had to make do with a ration of one packet of dried egg every two months, although children received double this amount.

Most people had to make do with one shilling and tuppence worth of meat each week, supplemented by canned American meats, such as Spam, Mor, and Prem, providing they had enough ration coupons to buy them. Horsemeat could be obtained if one knew where to go for it, but it was never popular with the British public, who, generally speaking, had the same sentimental attachment for horses as they have for dogs. Each individual also received a weekly ration of four ounces of bacon or ham; one-half pound of sugar; and one-half pound of fats, which was allocated in the proportion of two ounces of butter, two ounces of cooking fat or lard, and four ounces of margarine, the margarine being compulsory.

Cheese was rationed at one-half pound a week, but dropped to only two ounces in 1944. Jam or marmalade or mincemeat was rationed at the rate of one pound per person per month; and candy, at the rate of one-half pound per month. All tinned goods and dried peas and beans were rationed on what was known as the points system, so many "points" per can or pound.

Milk was rationed at one pint per day for children, invalids, pregnant women, and nursing mothers. The rest of the public was rationed to from two to four pints a week per head, depending on supplies. This was supplemented by National Dried Milk when it could be obtained. Bread, such as it was, was not rationed, nor were potatoes. Fresh fruit, though not rationed, was generally in short supply, as was fish, unrationed but scarce, because the Royal Navy had requisitioned most of the trawlers for patrol boats, minelayers, and sweepers.

Certain categories of workers, such as men in the heavy industries, in coal mining, and in agriculture, were given an extra cheese ration as a means of maintaining the protein that the nature of their work demanded.

The men of Britain's Merchant Navy fared better with regard to food than most people ashore, although nobody begrudged them this. After all, it was they who brought the food to Britain through submarine and mine-infested seas.

A certain class of British merchant seamen, known as weekly seamen because they signed weekly articles, were also given extra food allowances. Quite a number of these men hoarded their rations and took them ashore to their families. This, however, was illegal, and the men were fined when they were caught doing it. Seamen however, are naturally resourceful types, and the so-called weekly seamen devised a scheme to defeat the "nosy dock coppers" who stopped them to search their baggage when they went through the dock gates to their homes.

Somebody would catch the ship's cat or find a cat on the dockside and then put it in a large cardboard crate. carefully tied with rope. Then one of the crew, carrying the crate containing the resentful cat, would walk boldly up to the dock gate. Challenged by the dock policeman at the gate, the seaman would say that he had a cat in the box and that the cat was sick and he was taking it to a veterinary surgeon. The policeman would smile knowingly and say something to the effect that it was an unlikely tale and insist that the crate be opened.

After some argument, the man with the crate would unwillingly untie it and in doing so deliberately allow the now furiously indigant feline to escape and run off. Then the merchant seaman, in a fine show of righteous anger and indignation, would loudly berate the embarrassed policeman, saying that it was all his fault that the animal had escaped and now he, the seaman, would be put to all the trouble of going back to the ship to find it, catch it, and put it in the crate again.

Leaving the now apologetic policeman, the "indignant" seaman would go swearing off back to the ship again and, after a suitable period of time had elapsed, would return, clasping the well-tied crate. This time the policeman, far from insisting that the crate be opened, would say, "So you managed to catch it then?"

"Yes," the seaman would growl, "but no thanks to you. And this time he's *staying* caught." Then he would walk casually through the dock gate with the crate, now packed with hoarded rations. The cat-in-the-crate was an extremely successful subterfuge while it lasted, and it lasted for quite a considerable time.

Food in wartime Britain was more precious than gold, and, like gold, it had to be well-guarded.

On one occasion, the author, while on shore leave from the Merchant Navy, had been to the local food office to collect the National Dried Milk, orange juice, and cod-liver oil to which his eighteen-month-old daughter was entitled. This done, he went to the butcher shop to stand in the queue and wait for the family meat ration. While waiting, he was foolish enough to put his shopping bag on the floor; and when he picked it up again the milk, orange juice, and cod-liver oil had vanished as if by magic. Luckily for him, the manager of the food office believed his story and replaced the stolen items.

Queuing for food, supplies of which sometimes ran out even before she reached the counter, was but one of the wartime frustrations of the British housewife. Via the daily press and the BBC's "Kitchen Front," she was subjected to a barrage of "advice" from "food experts" that was often quite ridiculous.

She was admonished not to spoil vegetables by boiling them too much. "Let the children drink vegetable water," she was told by the "experts." "It will provide them with vitamins." It is doubtful if any of these "kitchen Front" pundits had ever tried to persuade children to drink cabbage water, but no matter. They still continued with their barrage of "advice." People who lived in the country were told to gather dandelion leaves for salads and informed that young nettles when boiled made an excellent substitute for spinach. It was a great pity that the "experts" did not mention the fact that rhubarb leaves were a deadly poison if boiled and eaten. If they had, they might well have saved at least one life.

British housewives and indeed the British public, generally, frequently found the broadcast advice of the Ministry of Food most irritating. For example, they were told: "Do not despise fish and chips. It is good, nourishing food." *Fish and chips* was a British institution anyway, and millions, especially in the poorer classes, had been raised on it practically from birth. Moreover, being told what to do with the leftovers from a weekly meat ration of one shilling and tuppence value merely added insult to injury.

One of the greatest social injustices at the beginning of the war was that restaurants could serve unrationed food. Thus the wealthy could eat out and so supplement their food rations, whereas the poorer people just had to make do on their basic rations.

However, during the London blitz, an excellent organization called the Londoners' Meal Service came into being. It provided wholesome meals at reasonable prices for those whose homes had been destroyed by bombing. From this organization emerged 2,160 British Restaurants, which provided well over half a million meals a day at the cost of about one shilling a meal.

As the war progressed, the Ministry of Labour encouraged and, in some instances, compelled factory managements to provide their workers with canteens where meals could be obtained at economic prices. At the end of the war, something like 19,000 of these factory canteens existed.

With such facilities as these, eating out to supplement basic rations became part of the wartime way of life, and by the end of the war something like 170 million meals a week were being eaten out.

11. Industry at War

EARLY IN THE WAR, Britain was in a truly desperate plight, for most of the nation's weapons, including heavy guns, tanks, and transport, had been left behind during the evacuation of Dunkirk.

Lord Beaverbrook, minister of aircraft, and Herbert Morrison, minister of supply, exhorted the nation's workers to work as they had never done before, for on their efforts depended Britain's survival.

The dynamic Lord Beaverbrook was obsessed to the exclusion of all else with the production of aircraft. As a result, Britain's aircraft production shot up at a fantastic rate, often at the expense of the health and well-being of the workers. Historians have said that this phenomenal production was only achieved at the cost of tank production and that if the enemy had succeeded in invading Britain in September 1940, the nation might well have been defeated then through its lack of tanks. As it was, Lord Beaverbrook's leadership in aircraft production undoubtedly prevented that invasion. Even before the premises of the Ministry of Aircraft Production were ready, Lord Beaver-

158

brook set up office in his London home, where he and his entire staff worked a ferociously demanding 18 hours a day. Ruthless and even tyrannical he may have been, but it was these qualties, together with his organizing and administrative abilities, that Britain needed to survive.

He gathered around him Britain's most high-powered and experienced industrial chiefs, with a team of equally high-powered journalists to write his propaganda. Prominent among Beaverbrook's leaders was Sir Charles Craven, chief of the great firm Vickers Armstrong; Mr. T. Westbrook of Supermarine, the name linked with the incomparable Spitfire plane; and Mr. P. Hennesy of the Ford Motor Company, who brought with him his own team of highly qualified industrialists.

The first thing this virile new ministry did was to give absolute priority to the production of Spitfire and Hurricane combat planes. History has confirmed the wisdom of this decision.

Lord Beaverbrook, whose tirelessness earned him the nickname "the Beaver," was no respecter of persons or traditions. His ability to improvise was staggering, and the power of his propaganda was such that he made every individual feel personally involved in the winning of the war. All managers of production plants had orders to report in full every day the shortages that were holding up production, and the manner in which these shortages were remedied was novel and probably unique.

Salvage operations were organized so efficiently and swiftly that materials and components from aircraft that had been shot down were back in the factories, sometimes within hours, to be incorporated in new aircraft. Maintenance units composed of skilled civilian personnel worked round the clock removing the wreckage of crashed and bombed aircraft from airfields to highly organized salvage dumps, where materials and components could be swiftly removed for reuse. On a 100-acre site near Oxford was a huge salvage dump, where the grim debris of destroyed aircraft was piled in great oblong heaps. Here teams of workers searched for and removed necessary parts and components needed for new planes.

Lord Beaverbrook, by means of the national daily press, which he was later to control, exhorted British house-wives to give him their aluminum pots, pans, and kettles so that they could be converted into combat planes and bombers. Everybody responded to this call, including the Royal Family, and the local offices of the Women's Voluntary Service (WVS) were inundated with great piles of aluminum kitchen utensils.

Nor was this all, for Lord Beaverbrook organized the famous "Buy a Spitfire" fund, and the money rolled in like a tide, not only from Britain, but from countries of the British Commonwealth. Eventually, the BBC was broad-casting the lists of donations, which totalled £13 million by April, 1941.

In addition to this, the government organized a National Savings Campaign to help finance the war and at the same time prevent inflation. Large sums of money were spent on propaganda urging the public to save money —not spend it. This propaganda included large posters showing the grotesque Squanderbug with pear-shaped head, pointed teeth, and suitably adorned with swastikas. The wording on the poster was clumsy and naive, declaring that the "Squanderbug, alias Hitler's pal" was known to be at large in certain part of the kingdom, "usually found in the company of useless articles, has a tempting leer and a flattering manner." However, in spite of such childish insults to their intelligence, the British people were saving money for the war effort.

Every Sunday, after the 6:00 P.M. news, the BBC broadcast "National Savings News," to which most people listened with interest. Spectacular "savings drives" were organized in Britain's towns and cities. In addition to the 'Buy a Spitfire' fund, there were War Weapons Weeks, Wings for Victory Week, Salute the Soldier Week, and Warships Weeks. In aid of the latter, the inhabitants of the Isle of Lewis in the remote Hebrides raised the remarkable sum of £270,000, remarkable because the majority of the islanders were fishermen and crofters or small farmers.

The man responsible for the War Savings Campaign was Sir Robert Kindersley, who had been head of the National Savings movement in peacetime. His organization was eminently successful, for eventually there were some 300,000 savings groups. These included school, factory, and neighborhood groups and others in the various branches of the Civil Defence. Proof of Sir Robert's success was the fact that in peace time the average savings per person was less than 5 percent after tax. Now it was about 25 percent. It must be noted, however, that these savings were due in some degree to the fact that there were now few luxuries to buy.

In May, 1941, Lord Beaverbrook resigned as minister of aircraft production and became minister of supply. His task now was that of tank production, to see to it that the hitherto underpowered and undergunned British tanks were replaced by tanks that could deal with those of the all-victorious panzers.

In the meantime, in spite of Herbert Morrison's exhortation "Go to it!", all was far from well in the ranks of Britain's war workers. Strikes were still prevalent, even though they were now illegal. To be sure, industrial disputes had fallen off during the fever of the Dunkirk evacuation, but by 1941 the man-hours lost through industrial disputes were creeping back to prewar levels. This was largely due to the traditional gulf, born of mutual distrust, which exists between workers and management and which even the exigencies of a war of survival could not bridge. The workers were still haunted by the ghosts of mass unemployment, which marked the 1930s and which they feared would again be part of the postwar scene.

Employers had their own misgivings. Concessions naturally had to be made to the workers during wartime, and the employers feared that these concessions would be the thin end of the wedge that would give the workers greater power after the war. The workers, on the other hand, feared that they would be deprived of these concessions when the war ended, and they were unwilling to abandon the restrictive practices they had used as a means for wage bargaining in peacetime. It was the old and bitter story. The war workers felt that they were not getting sufficient pay, whereas the employers felt that the workers' wages were too high already.

These circumstances were aggravated by the fact that many of Britain's skilled workers had been drafted into the armed forces and the war factories now were manned by old men, semi-invalids, men with criminal records, and even some mentally retarded.

To make up for the lack of skilled workers, government training centers were set up where boys and men too old for military service were trained to become skilled and semiskilled engineers. Something like 300,000 women were also trained in these centers, and for the first time in British history women were seen doing skilled, light engineering jobs and using welding equipment in the factories and shipyards. At first the men in the factories regarded these women as a glamourous novelty, but as the war went on this glamour wore off, and the men regarded them as a real threat to their jobs when the war was over.

The employment of women, however skilled, also posed problems for management. Many women workers had husbands and families, and to help deal with this problem local authorities organized day nurseries, where children could be cared for while their mothers were at work.

Time wasted standing in the food queues was another problem, for it not only added immeasurably to the burden of the worker-housewives, but also posed problems of absenteeism for the managements of factories. The more enlightened ones gave their women workers time off for this dreary but necessary chore.

These and other problems eventually prompted Ernest Bevin to compel factories with more than 250 workers to appoint special welfare officers to deal with the complaints and problems of both male and female workers. As a result, the working conditions of British factories began to improve generally. Staff canteens, sickrooms with trained medical staff permanently in attendance, and even rest rooms, together with piped-in "music while you work," became part of the wartime scene in industry.

Meanwhile, the coal mining industry had its own troubles. At the beginning of the war, Britain had something like a thousand coal mining companies employing 700,000 miners. There was discord already in the coalfields of Britain, for the evils of the past were still very close.

The miners were still thinking of the hardships and injustices they had endured because of outmoded and restricted monopolies and the cutthroat wage practices of the colliery owners. The miners remembered how, in the recent past, the larger coal mining companies had kept miners' wages to a bare subsistence level in order to produce cheap coal for Britain's iron, steel, and chemical industries. Moreover, the attack by the mine owners on the miners' wages was constant and unremitting. It was the miners' bitter resistance to this that had led to the disastrous General Strike in Britain in 1926.

The memories of the miners were long, for in October, 1943, Mr. Alex Sloane, M.P., in a bitter speech in the House of Commons reminded the members that Winston Churchill had led the capitalists against the miners, who, though they fought to the bitter end, were defeated. Aneurin ("Nye") Bevan, a member from the coalfields of South Wales, also attacked Churchill in the House.

Such recriminations were not calculated to help the British war industry, and the fact that Britain was fighting for her very existence did nothing to lessen the ancient hatreds and mistrust that existed between the miners and the mine owners. Nor was the situation made any better by the fact that the miners who were left to work the mines were aging and embittered men, while the younger miners who had joined the armed forces had no wish to return to the dangers and discomforts of the coal mines—now or ever.

At this period Britain's coal mines were controlled by the Mines Department of the Board of Trade and that control was recognized as inefficient. In 1942 the government stated that it would take over the coal mines, which would be reorganized as a national service. The truth was that the government did not take over the coal mines, but left the mine owners and their managements to run the industry much as they had run it in the past. The only immediate benefit came from temporarily increased production which was due to mechanization.

Gwilym Lloyd George, the minister of fuel and power, was far from satisfied with the operation of the coal mines and said that the only solution to the problem was a complete take-over of the mines by his ministry. Winston Churchill, however, refused to agree to this, although a few of the coal mines were taken over by the Ministry of Fuel and Power.

This take-over led to further bitterness among the miners of Priory Pit in Lanarkshire, Scotland, who refused to accept the ministry's new rate of pay and were locked out by the management as a result; this was also an illegal action. The miners returned unwillingly to work, not mollified in the least to know that in locking them out, the pit manager had contravened the Essential Works Order and had been fined £50.

In recent years, the economic expert Dr. Beeching has closed down a number of coal mines in Britain, but during the war every hundredweight of coal was vitally important to industry, bringing the Coal Charges Account into existence. By means of this, the profitable coal mines subsidized those that were not profitable. In spite of this and of increasing mechanization, Britain's coal output steadily declined, falling from 204 million tons in 1942 to 175 million tons in 1945, the last year of the war.

When the miners were blamed for this loss of output,

their bitterness increased; and so did the strikes, lockouts, fines, and jailings.

It was at Betteshanger Colliery Kent in 1941 that the most notable industrial dispute of the war occurred, one that made history. It must be established that this was no ordinary dispute. Hard and often embittered men though they were, the coal miners were as eager to see Hitler defeated as the rest of the British people. The trouble at the Betteshanger Colliery, which then employed 4,000 miners, was due to a coal seam that was difficult to work, owing to a stratum of what miners call muck. Because of this muck and the difficulty of working the seam, coal production fell at a time when Britain needed coal as never before.

The Betteshanger miners could not deliver the tonnage required of them, and because of this their wages fell. As a result, a dispute arose between the miners and Big Sam Magee, the mine manager. When this dispute could not be resolved, the miners and the mine management had to go before an arbitration court, headed by Sir Charles Doughty, who, according to the miners, had no knowledge of coal mining. Yet this arbitration was both compulsory and legally binding.

The findings of the court of arbitration crystallized the miners' feelings of hostility into action. It awarded them even lower wages than those that had been offered by the management and that had been the original cause of the dispute. To show their bitter resentment, they staged a slowdown at the colliery. The management retaliated by again lowering their wages, and the miners retaliated by going on strike.

At this point in the dispute, Winston Churchill and Lord Beaverbrook wanted to prosecute the Betteshanger miners. Ernest Bevin, the minister of labour, was now in a very unhappy position, for while there was undeniable friction between himself and Lord Beaverbrook, Bevin had a great loyalty towards Winston Churchill.

Bevin, the son of a Somerset farmhand, was a dedicated trade unionist and owed his loyalty to the miners also. Because of this, he tried to push the Betteshanger dispute aside, but to no avail; summonses were served on 1,000 of the Betteshanger miners, who pleaded guilty to a man.

Three of the miners, Joe Methuen, their union leader; William Powell; and Tudor Davies, were brought to trial in the city of Canterbury. They went there with the miners' brass band leading them and a special gasoline allowance for their automobiles. Joe Methuen was sentenced to one month's imprisonment, William Powell to two months' imprisonment and Tudor Davies * to one month, all with hard labor. In addition, 1,000 miners were fined one pound each, although only nine ever paid their fines.

Determined to show loyalty to their imprisoned friends, the Betteshanger miners refused to go back to work until they were released from jail. After three days, the three prisoners were released, and the findings of the court of arbitration were reversed in favor of the miners. Then the Betteshanger mines went back to work and within a short time had produced a record coal output.

It was a victory for the miners and a notable ending to an unusual industrial conflict, but there was infinitely more terrible strife raging in East Kent at this time.

---

* The author was acquainted with Tudor Davies in later years, and never was there a man less like the public concept of a militant miner. His thick, silvery hair, natural dignity, and fascinating Welsh intonation gave him the aura of an arch-Druid.

12. Hell's Corner

THE COUNTY OF Kent, England, is separated from the coast of France by a mere 21-mile-wide strip of sea—the famous Strait of Dover. This part of England since earliest prehistoric times has seen both folk migration and invasion. Scattered far and wide over the chalky downlands are the relics of the ancient peoples who came and went or were absorbed into the British race. Everywhere are Stone Age, Bronze Age, Iron Age, Roman, Saxon, and Norman dwelling sites, burial grounds, and tumuli. The whole place has a sense of movement and in some places a strange and unaccountable atmosphere of menace left by battles so ancient that even the people who live there have forgotten them.

In the tiny village of Kingsdown near Dover, during the Napoleonic Wars, local fishermen worked at their nets and in their boats by day, but at night withdrew to the inland village of Ringwold for fear of French landing parties.

During World War II this part of Britain was again the nearest land to the enemy, and it was so continuously under attack that it became known as Hell's Corner. Here, more than anywhere else, people were suspicious of the deadly fifth column.

Major Pratt-Boorman, a well-known figure in East Kent and proprietor of the county newspaper *Kent Messenger*, stopped to ask an old countryman the way to a village whose signpost had been removed.

"Aye, I know," growled the old peasant, "but I'm not going to tell you. You may be one o' they danged fifth columnists for all I know."

Right from the beginning, Hell's Corner had been in the very center of the ferocious aerial Battle of Britain. Hundreds of German aircraft were shot down here, and sometimes the German pilots who survived received gentler treatment than they merited.

One Luftwaffe pilot was shot down in a hop field near Collier Street, Kent, and surrendered formally, speaking in perfect English to a farmer who was plowing a nearby field, indifferent to the shell splinters, bullets, and the planes that came crashing down around him. The farmer looked at the German pilot and said mildly, "I suppose you had better come up to my house." While they waited for the police to come, the farmer and his wife gave the pilot a cup of tea from their tiny weekly ration.

The aerial fighting over Hell's Corner was tremendous. On July 29, 1940, 80 enemy bombers attacked Dover Harbor, bombing ships and harbor installations. Seventeen of these aircraft were shot down in an attack so violent that the censor allowed Dover to be mentioned in the national news, a practice hitherto forbidden as it gave information to the enemy.

In complete contrast to this vicious but costly attack

was the dropping by a lone German bomber of thousands of propaganda leaflets on August 10, 1940; they were entitled "Hitler's last appeal to reason to the British people." This caused tremendous amusement throughout the whole of Britain, for the leaflets fell on Kent's Barming Hospital for the mentally deficient.

As these leaflets merely aroused the derision of the stubborn British, the Luftwaffe decided to teach them a lesson they would not forget. On August 12, 1940, Dover was attacked by 11 waves of Nazi bombers, 200 aircraft in all, which bombed the harbor and the ships and shot down the balloons of the balloon barrage. It was the Germans, however, who were taught a lesson, for they lost 61 aircraft in this raid.

Other bombers deliberately dropped incendiary bombs into the fields of grain growing all around Dover and district, but the grain was not ripe, and the fiercely spluttering bombs just sizzled out at last, leaving nothing but small circles of ash. Detling Airfield in Kent was attacked by 30 Junkers bombers with a strong escort of ME 109 combat planes, and in this raid many RAF personnel were killed and injured.

This was the period when the Battle of Britain was raging in its full terrible fury and when the tide of that battle was turning in Britain's favor. Between August 8 and August 18, 1940, the Luftwaffe lost 697 aircraft for the loss of 153 British aircraft, and Hell's Corner was one vast funeral pyre of wrecked aircraft.

And it was on August 18 that hell was truly let loose in Hell's Corner. The blue dome of the sky was one vast, raging battleground crossed and recrossed with the white vapor trails of hundreds of planes diving, swooping, weav-

ing as they locked in furious combat. The warm air rocked
and quivered to the howl of diving planes, the roaring
whine of engines, and the tearing blast of machine-gun and
20-mm cannon fire. Shattered planes howled from the sky
like smoking, flaming meteors bursting into great rose-red
blossoms of fire as they hit the earth. And the sky was
dotted with the parachutes of pilots and aircrews, both
British and German, whose planes had been shot down, but
who were lucky enough to live through the holocaust.

Many of the bombers managed to drop their bombs,
and thousands of houses in Hell's Corner were destroyed
or badly damaged. But the people who had lost their
homes just planted Union Jacks on the heaps of rubble to
show their defiance. Others wrote amusing slogans and
put them on their damaged premises. Shopkeepers whose
windows had been blown out covered the gaping holes
with sheets of tarred canvas on which were written such
comments as "I have no pane, dear mother, now," a parody
on the words of an old song entitled "I have no pain, dear
mother, now." Another slogan read: "My pane is gone,
but Hitler has one in the neck." Less imaginative but
equally undaunted shopkeepers just put up notices "Business as usual" and displayed their goods in their glassless
windows. One whose shop was near to a huge, unexploded
bomb with a delayed action fuse put up a notice: "No
delayed action here" and went on serving his customers.
A boot and shoe mender, whose shop had been damaged
and who was a member of the Air Raid Precaution (ARP)
put up a notice

A . . . ll
R . . . epairs
P . . . roceeding

The great French tyrant Napoleon Buonaparte once scornfully described the British as "a nation of shop-keepers," but if he could have met *these* shopkeepers, he would have revised his opinion.

On August 26, 1940, the seaside holiday town of Ramsgate, a few miles north of Dover, was badly bombed. Many houses and shops and five pubs were destroyed and damaged. Ramsgate Assembly Hall was completely destroyed, but a notice on what was left of the charred and blackened walls said, "Cheer up. The best part of history is still to be written."

A Ramsgate baker's roundsman was delivering bread to his customers when the house he was about to go to received a direct hit from a bomb and vanished before his eyes. The baker's van was also demolished, and the loaves of bread were blown all over the road. By a miracle, the roundsman was unharmed, and after he had pulled the family of the wrecked house unharmed from the ruins, he scooped up a loaf of bread from the road and gave it to them.

The civilian casualties in Ramsgate were comparatively light, for Ramsgate Town Council had been farsighted in their concern for the safety of the inhabitants. They had spent £60,000 in cutting deep and spacious tunnels in the solid chalk beneath the town; something like 6,000 people lived almost permanently in these tunnels. Hundreds of families set up homes of canvas-walled cubicles in the electrically lit tunnels and lived, ate, and slept there almost as comfortably as they had done in their homes above ground.

These tunnels undoubtedly saved many lives for Ramsgate, like most other towns on the southern, southeastern, and eastern coasts of England, suffered the scourge of the "sneak raider," also called hit-and-run raiders. These were sometimes bombers, sometimes combat planes, that came singly or in twos and threes, hurtling out of low clouds, fog, or mist to drop their bombs at random and machine-gun anything and anybody in sight.

In a sense, living on the coast was worse than living inland in towns and cities, for in those there was almost always a warning on the air raid sirens before the attack developed. On the coast, there was rarely time to give warning before the raiders roared in, sometimes so low they seemed to touch the wave tops.

In spite of this constant threat the morale of the people in Hell's Corner was very high indeed, and this was manifest at the town of Sittingbourne when an ME 109 combat plane had been shot down. A large crowd had assembled to look at the pilot, who had bailed out safely, and the special police on duty took advantage of the situation to hand collection boxes among the crowd for donations to Lord Beaverbrook's Spitfire fund.

While the fighter pilots of the RAF were making history in the skies above Hell's Corner, the crews of the anti-aircraft batteries were also giving a good account of themselves. In one Kentish village a 22-year-old gunner working a 40-mm Bofors gun blasted three Dornier bombers out of the sky in one minute flat. So fast did he fire that a continuous rain of debris and bombs from the shattered bombers fell like destructive hail, damaging many houses and the Farningham School for boys. By a miracle nobody was killed.

At the village of Marden in this beleaguered corner of England, one antiaircraft gunner armed with nothing more formidable than an ancient .303 Lewis gun of World

War I vintage, tensely watched a duel between a Spitfire and an ME 109. The enemy plane swooped low to evade the Spitfire, and the next instant the Lewis gunner had riddled its fuel tank with an incredibly swift and accurate burst of fire. The ME 109 came down, otherwise intact, in a field, where its 26-year-old pilot was taken prisoner just as he was about to set fire to his plane.

The pilot of another ME 109, after having had his plane shot away from under him by antiaircraft gunners in the town of Maidstone, Kent, landed by parachute and surrendered to members of the Home Guard. "Well done, Spitfires," he said in English to Home Guard Captain A. H. Terry. He was extremely humiliated the next minute when Captain Terry told him he had fallen victim to the guns of the ground defenses.

The larger groups and formations of the Luftwaffe and their combat plane escorts usually left the smaller towns and villages unharmed as they thundered in over the southeastern coast to bomb London and its suburbs. Living in a small country village or town was no guarantee of safety, however, for the market town of Ashford, Kent, was bombed by a single raider on the evening of September 16, 1940. and an entire row of houses was wrecked and two people killed. On September 6, Ashford was again attacked by a lone bomber, which demolished four houses and killed three people.

All over this exposed southeastern corner of England, towns and villages were being bombed, apparently at random and with no other purpose than to terrorize the countryfolk.

The gracious, old-world town of Tonbridge Wells in Kent was devastated by fire when enemy bombers dropped canisters of incendiary bombs known as Molotov bread-baskets. In this fire raid shops, houses, the police station, the assembly hall, a motion-picture theater, newspaper offices, pubs, and a £10,000 sports pavilion were gutted out by fire bombs.

But the courage of the people of Tonbridge Wells never faltered, nor did their sense of humor. The owner of a burnt-out grocery store, which had been destroyed by fire in a previous raid and rebuilt, hung a notice outside the charred wreckage of his shop "Second round. Still not out."

The enemy attacks on Hell's Corner went on. Bombs fell on the town of Sittingbourne, demolishing and damaging houses, shops, a church, and a garage and killing eight people and wounding many others.

Maidstone was bombed by two squadrons of bombers; and houses, business premises, churches, chapels, restaurants, shops, and Maidstone Museum were destroyed and damaged. Many people were killed and injured, but like the other folk who lived in Hell's Corner, the inhabitants of Maidstone had fighting hearts. So splendidly did the Maidstone ARP personnel deal with the grim and tragic situation that the chairman of Kent County Council sent the following official letter to Sir Garrad Tyrwhitt-Drake, chief of the Kent ARP:

> I was filled with admiration not only with the way the various ARP services functioned but with the calm, courageous manner in which the people accepted the situation.

This letter could well have been written for the entire British people. And it was this indomitable spirit that was already driving Hitler into the mad excesses of vengeance and murder that contributed to much to the downfall of the Third Reich.

And always and ever amid the danger, the ruins, the stench of death, destruction, and burned high explosive lurked the people's unquenchable humor.

Bombs caused other troubles beside destruction and death. During a night raid on the wealthy, residential town of Chiselhurst, Kent, a bomb exploded outside a house. The house was not demolished, but every pane of glass in the windows was blown out, and the blast somehow switched on all the lights. The lights blazed out from every gaping window, and as enemy bombers were directly overhead, the townsfolk immediately assumed that the house was the abode of fifth columnists, who were signaling the raiders. In spite of the falling bombs and general uproar, a furiously angry mob gathered outside the house, prepared to lynch anyone who might come out. So furious was the mob that a riot ensued; and the police, unable to control it, called upon a local magistrate, Colonel Edlman, to read the Riot Act and disperse the rioters, who were causing a public disturbance the like of which the eminently respectable town of Chiselhurst had never seen before. No copy of the Riot Act could be found; and while Colonel Edlman was trying to remember enough of it to deliver to the rioters, the police broke into the house, which proved to be empty. Unable to find the switches, they broke all the bulbs of the offending lights. The rioters, now satisfied that there were no fifth columnists, went back to their homes.

The pattern of wartime life in Hell's Corner and the rest of the exposed southern, southeastern, and eastern coasts was different from that of the big inland towns and cities. In the latter, daylight raids were not too common; and when night fell, the people would go to their shelters as a matter of routine. In Hell's Corner and the rest of the exposed coastal areas, one had to be constantly on the alert. A "sneak raider" would come hurtling in at low level long before any air raid alert could be sounded, drop its bombs, rake the vicinity with machine-gun and cannon fire, and then be gone before it could be intercepted.

It was a nerveracking existence at first, but eventually people became inured to it, and even the reflexes of old people improved astonishingly. At the first sound of a roaring engine nobody stopped to look up to see if it was "one of ours" or "one of theirs." They just dived headlong for cover and afterwards proudly pointed out the bullet holes and bomb splinter holes in their automobiles.

When the sound of an approaching aircraft was heard, cyclists and pedestrians would jump into the nearest ditch and lie flat. Drivers stopped their automobiles and did likewise. Milkmen dived into the house where they were delivering, if they could; or failing that, they dived to cover underneath their milk floats. Farmers and farmhands threw themselves flat in their fields or under their tractors if they were using them.

As time went on, people became so inured to danger that they just went on doing whatever it was until the sound of the aircraft engine grew too close for comfort. Country people found that by watching the flight of flocks of birds they could tell if aircraft were in the vicinity, even before they could hear them.

Foremost among the everyday heroes of Britain were the stalwarts who kept the country's railways working, in spite of constant attacks on trains, railways lines, stations and signal towers, and railway marshalling yards.

A Kent stationmaster said, "We had no shelters, and if things got too hot, we'd stop the train and dive into a ditch, under a platform, anywhere. We often took a stupid risk watching our pilots chasing Jerries. It was like the front seat of a really good show."

It was not always "entertainment" for the railway men, who sometimes found themselves cast in the role of "actors" in the "show."

Motorman (train driver) Mr. F. Smith, who drove electric trains between Maidstone and the London terminus, Victoria Station, was driving his train through the station of a place called Blickley just as the station received a direct hit from a bomb. The train was battered with flying glass, hurtling bricks, and debris and had most of its windows broken, but it did not stop.

As the battered train approached Swanley Station, Kent, a canister of incendiary bombs whistled down, burst on the track in front of the train, and set fire to the tar-soaked wooden railway sleepers. Mr. Smith drove on through the sheet of flames right into the path of another shower of incendiary bombs, which again set the sleepers on fire. Others crashed through the roof of the second coach, luckily empty.

As the train drove into Swanley Station, rocking with the blast of bombs exploding all round and concentrated antiaircraft fire, Mr. Smith found the station deserted, for the station staff and the waiting passengers had wisely taken cover.

The train started off again, its only passengers being some young soldiers who were singing to keep their spirits up and a young mother with a baby, who was so terrified that Mr. Smith took her and her baby into the driver's cab with him to comfort her.

As they approached Wrotham Station, Kent, traveling at 60 miles an hour, another heavy bomb exploded near the track and almost blew the train off the rails. But Mr. Smith kept going, and the train arrived at Maidstone only ten minutes late. The men of British Railways got their trains through as long as there were lines to run them on.

The hazard of long-range shelling from the German-occupied coast of France across the 21 miles of the Strait of Dover was an additional danger faced by hte towns of Dover, Deal, Walmer, and the villages and hamlets in the immediate vicinity. This particular part of Hell's Corner had the additional name of Hellfire Corner, and with good reason. In a sense, it was in a position similar to the city of Atlanta during the American Civil War, for it was the target of a massive concentration of siege guns. Never in the entire history of Britain did one single part of the country face such a fearsome array of gigantic cannon.

At Cap Blanc Nez stood the Lindemann Battery, whose three mighty 406-mm guns, mounted on railway tracks and nicknamed Adolf, could hurl a 1,500-lb shell to a distance of 57,000 yards.

Near Cap Griz Nez stood the Todt Battery of four 381-mm guns, each weighing 320 tons, mounted on railway tracks and capable of hurling their great projectiles to a distance of 60,500 yards.

At Wimereaux stood the Friedrich Auguste Battery of 305-mm guns, which fired 880-lb shells to a distance of 60,500 yards, with smaller guns, which fired a 308-lb shell to 11,000 yards and which were used against British shipping.

At Cherbourg stood the Hamburg Battery of four

long-range guns, the details of which are not available, and the Marcouf Battery of three 210-mm guns, said to have been captured from the French.

The heavier guns of greater range bombarded Dover and the towns and villages in the vicinity while the shorter-range guns concentrated on any Allied shipping within range. And no ship was too small for the fearful attention of these batteries.

Just before D Day, the author was aboard a lightship being towed through the Strait of Dover by a small tender to mark one of the Normandy beachheads for the coming Allied invasion of Europe. It was a fine day, the sea, smooth; and the visibility, good—far too good for safety. As the towing vessel and her charge drew abreast of Dover, about five miles out, a German spotter plane flew over and had soon radioed the range of the tender and the lightship to the German shore batteries.

Within a short time, the salvos of great shells, five at a time, began hurtling overhead with a blood-chilling "swish-swish . . . swish-swish . . . swish-swish." The accuracy of the German gunners was terrifying; the third salvo fell so close that the funnel of the tender was riddled with shell splinters.

In all probability, the two small vessels would have been bown out of the water but for the timely aid of Royal Naval motor launches led by an old-fashioned biplane, which sped out from Dover and laid a smoke screen round the tender and its tow.

The first time Dover was shelled was on December 12, 1940, and it is said that the worst experiences of the entire war for the inhabitants of Dover were caused by these giant shells, which howled down from a height of 40,000 feet at supersonic speeds.

At this time, a strange rumor was current that Germany had exhausted its supply of bombs and that high-flying enemy bombers were dropping shells instead. One London newspaper, at least, published news to this effect, but American newspapers told the true story when they stated that the shells that had fallen on Dover had been fired by a 12 in caliber gun, possibly of French origin.

When the long, jagged splinters of the shells from this salvo, which had killed a man and a woman and wrecked a number of houses, were examined by experts, they confirmed that the American press had been right. The inhabitants of Dover were very annoyed at this, for they felt that the British press had let them down.

Ten days after the first shelling of Dover, a convoy of 18 British merchant ships passing through the Strait of Dover was bombed and shelled continuously for two hours. Hundreds of Britons watched the attack from the tops of the chalk cliffs of Dover, just as their ancestors of 2,000 years before had watched the approaching ships of the Romans led by Julius Caesar. The watchers cheered mightily as they saw the convoy steam on, unharmed, through the smoke and waterspouts of bursting shells and bombs. The efforts of the German gunners were both ineffectual and costly, for they fired a total of 145 heavy shells costing £100,000 to no purpose.

As the convoy continued on its way past the town of Deal, it was attacked by German JU 87 dive bombers, which were chased off by combat planes of the RAF after one dive bomber had been destroyed.

On the evening of that same day, just after 9 o'clock, another salvo of three giant shells screeched down on old Dover town. This was followed shortly after by a further salvo of nine shells.

Although a great deal of damage was done to houses and buildings and a number of people were killed and wounded, the Dovorians showed no signs of panic. They did, however, say that they thought that being shelled was worse than being bombed. "You never know where the next shell is going to fall, like you do with bombs" one of the townsfolk said.

In time the people of Dover became so used to being shelled and bombed that they could instantly tell the difference between an exploding shell and an exploding bomb. The former was a gigantic "Whoof!" and the latter a duller, heavier "Crump!" In fact, many of the Dovorians at last became so used to being shelled that they would stand on the cliff tops watching the great flashes of the German guns and making guesses and even bets as to where the shells would fall.

In time it was discovered that the damage caused by a 1,500-lb shell was less than that caused by a 1,000-lb bomb. This made it more difficult to locate the exact spot where a shell had fallen, although if it hit a house or brick-building, the immediate sign of the hit was a tall column of red dust from pulverized bricks.

All through the war the shells continued to fall on Dover and the immediate district at sporadic intervals. One shell passed through the stained-glass window of St. Barnabas Church, Dover, and gutted the interior without demolishing the structure. Another blew the back off an Anderson air raid shelter, but did no harm to the family who was sheltering there. A coastal village near Dover had three houses wrecked by a shell. In the kitchen of one totally demolished house, rescue workers found the remains of a shattered basin standing on a table. The eggs that the basin had contained were unbroken—another example of the freakish effect of high-explosive blast.

The long-range shelling was merely an expensive and ineffectual form of terrorism, which did nothing but stiffen the resolve of the hard-pressed Dover people. In time they took it for granted, and the only indication that the town was under bombardment was the sounding of two air raid warnings on the siren instead of one as for bombing. The official notices in the streets that stated, "Shelling in progress" drew as little attention as peacetime notices declaring, "Road works in progress."

It can be truthfully said that the long-range shelling of Dover caused more concern to the rest of Britain than it did to those who were enduring it. Nevertheless, the bombardment took an inevitable toll of victims, and one of the most notable of these was Mr. C. H. Beaufoy, who had been chief magistrate of Dover during World War I and now at 73 was Dover's chief of special constables. Described in the British national press as "Dover's Grand Old Man," Mr. Beaufoy was blown from his bicycle by an exploding shell, and though permanently blinded, he continued to play an important part in Dover's Air Raid Precaution services. To a newspaper reporter who visited him in St. Dunstan's Hospital for the Blind, Mr. Beaufoy said, "As soon as I have finished my rehabilitation training, I am going back to Dover. Of course, I am slightly handicapped, but I shall put on my uniform and lead the Victory Parade."

The towns of Deal and Walmer, near Dover, were also well within range of the German guns, and between October 5, 1942, and September 26, 1944, 127 German shells fell on them. The casualties were light, however: 12

killed, 13 seriously wounded, and 40 slightly wounded, with 39 buildings totally destroyed and several hundred badly damaged.

Deal's blackest day was January 20, 1944, when a salvo of four shells killed 12 people, seriously injured seven, and destroyed 12 houses. During the bombardment, a surface air raid shelter in Robert Street, Deal, received a direct hit from a shell, and ten people were killed instantly. The other two victims were Mr. and Mrs. Ernest Adams, who died when their bar, Park Tavern, received a direct hit and was completely demolished.

The German gun batteries that threatened the people of Hellfire Corner were linked by telephone to observation posts with large-scale maps of Dover and district plainly marked, but the primary task of the German batteries was to keep the Strait of Dover closed to British and Allied shipping. In this they failed completely, for the British were hitting back, and hitting hard.

While the German batteries, hidden in woods, heavily camouflaged, and under the cover of their own antiaircraft batteries, were blasting at British targets, British bombing planes frequently blasted the German gun sites.

In addition, the British had some gigantic, long-range guns of their own, which shelled the Nazis from gun emplacements hewn deep in the chalk of Dover cliffs. There were two groups of these giant, long-range guns: one group consisted of anti-invasion guns, and the other was known as counterbatteries, used for engaging the German long-range cannon. Even today not a great deal is known about these British guns.

One of these monstrous pieces of artillery was named Boche-buster, and its crew lived in a converted railway coach beside the gun emplacement rails, which can be seen to this day. Another of these huge engines of death and destruction had the unlikely name of Winnie-the-Pooh. The mightiest of them all and the biggest gun in the whole of Britain was named Winnie after Winston Churchill. Manned night and day by gun crews of Royal Marines; Winnie, with an old boot tied to its cavernous muzzle for luck, hurled its enormous shells to a height of nine miles before they howled down onto the German batteries.

On July 19, 1941, in the midst of a group of awed press photographers, reporters, and BBC technicians, Winnie's thunderous bellow was broadcast to the entire British nation as a morale booster.

The batteries of the huge British guns were no less complex and highly organized than the enemy batteries they struck back at. To begin with, a little-known and little-publicized Special Survey Regiment kept close watch night and day on the Nazi batteries across the Strait of Dover.

The technicians of this hush-hush regiment worked in teams of eight round the clock and within seconds of the firing of a German battery and by means of a recording device produced a strip of film showing the exact time the microphones of the recorder had received the sound of the German guns. With this and other data, a "reader," a "booker," and a "plotter" of the Survey Regiment then fixed the positions of the enemy batteries within a few yards.

This information was then swiftly passed to the gun crews, who returned the fire and then, by a method known as *sound ranging and flash spotting* with delicate and accurate instruments, the men of the Survey Regiment pinpointed the explosions of the British shells.

In these hazardous and dangerous times, it was very

unwise to get close to, or ask questions about, the giant British guns, whose massive, labyrinthine concrete emplacements still glower seawards from the heights of Langdon Cliffs, Dover, like the eye sockets of monstrous skulls. Frank Illingworth, the well-known reporter, who witnessed every German shelling of Dover, was arrested several times for showing too keen an interest in the great complex of gun batteries. On two occasions, he was marched by a military escort to the headquarters of British Intelligence, hewn deep in the 300-ft chalk cliffs, where he was severely reprimanded.

Another famous newspaperman who witnessed the shelling of Dover was the American war correspondent, Guy Murchie, who was wounded in the first simultaneous shelling and bombing of the ancient town. Mr. Murchie refused to have his wounds dressed until he had telephoned his war dispatch to London. This dispatch made journalistic history, for it is still regarded as one of the most sensational of the entire war.

Today one can still see maps of Dover and the other towns and villages of Hellfire Corner that show where the German shells fell, including the "black areas," where more than 12 shells fell within the radius of 100 yards.

These maps just show the outlines of the shells at the places where they fell, but the real picture was infinitely more harrowing and terrible: areas of total destruction, with piles of rubble where buildings and houses had once stood; the ripped-up roads covered with broken glass, clanging fire appliances, police cars, and ambulances; the shell-shocked, the wounded, and the dead; and over it all the stench of burnt high explosive, charred wet wood, and the tall, swirling red clouds of pulverized brickdust from the demolished houses.

Today the only relics of the carnage are the deep shell splinter marks on walls and buildings; the grass-grown shell craters on the downlands and in the fields; and the long, jagged, rusty shell splinters, which are still turned up by the plow.

13. The Battle For the Home Seas

THE COMMENCEMENT OF the battle for the home seas of England is notable for a blindly stupid atrocity that is unique in the annals of maritime history. It was the bombing and sinking of the unarmed English lightships, which marked the dangerous shoals and sandbanks of England's east coast and the approaches to the Thames Estuary.

Until the Spitfires and Hurricanes of RAF Fighter Command had smashed much of the power of the Luftwaffe, it was master of the air over the southern North Sea, the English Channel, and the shoal-haunted waters of the Thames Estuary, which, in effect, is a sunken delta.

Just as the crews of the lightships, which marked the numerous navigational hazards of these places, had seen the going and the coming of the incredible fleet that succored the men of Dunkirk, so they witnessed the fury of the Luftwaffe unleashed on British merchant shipping.

The North Goodwin lightship marks the northerly extremity of the infamous, ten-mile-long Goodwin Sands off the cost of East Kent. One warm and sunny day in the early summer of 1940, its crew stood watching a large convoy of ships passing close by. A few minutes later, the whole sky was filled with the drumming roar of bombers' engines, and a little later the whole world seemed to be engulfed in the swish and whistle of falling bombs. The entire seabed seemed to lift in a forest of giant black waterspouts with fire at their hearts and yellow smoke on their towering crests. A blinding orange flash enveloped the bridge of a big freighter, which wheeled in a slow circle like a blinded beast before it vanished beneath the filthy, churned-up sea, dotted with the white bellies of myriads of fish killed by the exploding bombs. A second merchant ship simply vanished in a great, billowing, black cloud of smoke and flame and flying debris. As the remainder of the convoy steamed on, the crew of the lightship lowered a boat to pick up survivors. There were none.

Owing to the fact that the lightships marked some of the world's most treacherous navigational hazards, the lightships remained at their stations to face the manifold dangers of the war at sea, *unarmed*. The crews were left alone to keep their desolate and dangerous watches, rescuing British and German aircrews impartially, and impotently watching the greet fleets of German bombers as they thundered remorselessly towards London. And the worst ordeal that the lightship men had to endure was the dreadful thought that their wives and families were living somewhere beneath the hellish glare in the night sky that marked distant London.

None of the lightshipmen, especially the older men with long service, ever believed for a moment that the lightships would ever be deliberately attacked. They might be blown up by stray mines or accidental bombs, but they would not be attacked, for they were there for the safety of all, friend or enemy, who might be in peril of the sea.

Only once in the three centuries of British history had the coastal lights of Britain been interfered with by an enemy power. At a time when Britain warred with France, the captain of a French frigate had captured workmen who were helping to erect the famous Eddystone lighthouse off the southwest coast of England. The captain of the frigate had proudly presented his prisoners to King Louis XIV of France, expecting praise and reward. All he received was a furious reprimand from the outraged king, who shouted, "Return them to their lighthouse instantly. I war with England, not with humanity!"

That the Nazis had no such scruples was soon made evident. One morning the lightship crews heard Lord Haw Haw broadcasting from Bremen. He said, "English lightships of the Thames Estuary have fired on aircraft of the Third Reich and will now be regarded as legitimate objectives of our bombers. Heil Hitler!"

The lightshipmen just laughed. "More propaganda," they said. How could they possibly fire at anything when, at that time, they did not have so much as a rifle to sink a floating mine? They did not laugh for long.

One sunny afternoon, the crew of the North Goodwin lightship was called up by radio from Ramsgate Coastguard Station: "North Goodwin. North Goodwin. Ramsgate calling. We have a message for you. Over."

"Hullo, Ramsgate. Hullo, Ramsgate. North Goodwin all attention. Over."

"Hullo, North Goodwin. Hullo, North Goodwin. Ramsgate answering. We regret that the South Folkestone Gate lightship has been sunk by enemy action. There were casualties. Ramsgate over and out."

Not long after this, Hermann Goering summoned the two Luftwaffe air aces Galland and Moelders to his Wagnerian residence, Karenhall, north of Berlin. During the meeting Goering admonished his two officers, telling them to bomb British aircraft factories "and not the Dover lightship." Fat Hermann had his facts wrong. He was referring to the South Folkstone Gate lightship.

At that time the author was one of the crewmen of the North Goodwin lightship and, while on shore leave, heard the story of the sinking of the South Folkestone Gate from Mr. James Eaton, who had been the lightship's master.

Five men of the crew of seven of the lightship had been below, eating their midday meal, leaving crewmen Jack Wade and Harry North on deck on watch. Suddenly six Dornier bombers, flying not much more than masthead height, swept in, to attack. The first bomber dropped two bombs, which missed, and at the same time raked the unarmed lightship with machine-gun fire, so that armor-piercing bullets drilled through the iron deck plating into the cabin where the men were eating, although nobody was hit.

One of the men on watch just had time to shout, "Look out, lads. We're being attacked!" before the second plane dropped its bombs, which also missed.

Then, as the men below were scrambling up the ladder to the deck, the third plane dropped its bombs. There was a terrible blast that seemed to lift the little 300-ton lightship clean out of the water, and then she heeled right over on her side with awful suddeness. Mr. Eaton heard the sea gushing into the sinking ship like the gurgling of a giant waste pipe.

Unaware that he had been caught by blast, Mr. Eaton, the blood streaming down his face, rushed to a bullet-riddled lifeboat to lower it. There were only two, and the other had been blown to pieces. As he struggled with the lifeboat. Mr. Eaton was shocked at what he saw. Water was rushing through a gaping hole in the lightship's side, the iron deckhouse was nothing but a heap of torn and smoking metal, and of crewmen Jack Wade and Harry North nothing remained except part of a shoulder with an arm attached. Mr. Eaton kicked this through the shattered bulwarks, hoping that the others had not seen it.

Thus the sea claimed all that remained of Jack Wade, whose generosity and never-failing good humor had made him one of the most popular men in the Trinity House Lightship Service.

The five shocked and dazed survivors managed to scramble along the tilting, hideously smeared deck and lower the damaged lifeboat, which was only kept afloat by its buoyancy tanks. Then, as they climbed into it, their lightship mercifully vanished beneath the bomb-churned sea.

Mr. Eaton's face had been badly gashed by innumerable tiny pieces of flying metal. As he leaned over the boat's side to wash the blood and grime from his face, he received a second hideous shock; for the water he was scooping up was foul with the shredded remains of the two men he had known and liked for many years. He said afterwards that this was his most terrible moment in the whole shocking incident.

In the meantime, a fast rescue launch was racing out from Dover and took the five survivors from the riddled lifeboat just before it sank. The outrage of the South Folkestone Gate lightship was only the beginning of a series of similar atrocities.

The East Dudgeon lightship some 20 miles off the lonely Norfork coast was also bombed and machine-gunned. The crew were unharmed, but the lightship was so badly damaged that it was decided to abandon her. The crew took to one of the small lifeboats and, in constant danger of being swamped, rowed all night through a driving blizzard and high seas toward the distant shore. They reached the coast at dawn, but were so exhausted with rowing and so weak from exposure to the bitter cold that they could not handle their boat in the mountainous surf along the shore. The boat capsized in the roaring breakers alongshore, and only one man of the crew of seven crawled up the cruel, snow-clad beach. His name was Richard Saunders. The bodies of the others were found scattered like flotsam along the shore.

The Sunk Lightship off Harwick on the coast of Essex was riddled with machine-gun and cannon fire and had to be withdrawn from her station. Luckily, the crew remained unharmed during the attack. The Trinity House lightship tender *Reculver* was bombed and machine-gunned and one of her officers blown to pieces as he tried to lower a lifeboat. The Trinity House tender *Argus* was sunk in the Thames Estuary with only one of her crew of 40 surviving.

One clear and sunny afternoon the crew of the North Goodwin watched a Valhalla of enemy bombers, with their swarming escort of combat planes, roaring remorselessly up-Thames. "London is for it again," said one of the crewmen hoarsely, and then the whole seabed seemed to leap as if an earthquake were imminent. A few seconds later came a rolling thunderous concussion that shocked the lightship-men to silence.

The Valhalla of German bombers had not released

The hole made by bomb in deck of Trinity House lightship tender *Reculver*, October, 1940.

their bombs on London. Instead they had dropped the entire bombload on No. 60 Lightship in the Thames Estuary—a lightship even smaller than the 300-ton North Goodwin. No. 60 and her crew were atomized, for nothing of the lightship or the men aboard her was ever seen again.

The next victim was the East Goodwin lightship marking the eastern extremity of the Goodwin Sands. She was attacked by Stukas, and the crew of the North Goodwin watched her vanish in a forest of bomb spouts. Luckily, the crew, who were billeted at Dover, were not aboard her at the time.

The South Goodwin lightship, which marks the southern extremity, just vanished overnight. Nobody saw her go. Again the crew were lucky, for they had been evacuated.

The North Goodwin was the only lightship left on that hazardous southeastern corner of England, with her crew wondering why they had been left and beginning to wonder if they had been forgotten in the chaos and confusion of the threatened invasion.

The sea around the lone lightship was a deadly battleground now with aerial combat raging overhead most of the time.

A Hurricane hurtled in among six ME 109s before the enemy knew what happened and smashed two down into the sea right alongside the lightship. The crew got ready to rescue the pilots, but only the wreckage of the two MEs came to the surface. Then the Hurricane ran out of ammunition, and the four surviving enemy combat planes turned on it savagely. A tempest of machine-gun fire hammered the lone British plane in the air, and the lightship crew saw pieces flying from it and a great gush of gasoline spout from the tank as it roared past, only 20 or so yards away. They saw, too, the stony faces of the German pilots of the pursuing enemy planes and the jets of orange flame from their guns.

The pilot of the badly damaged Hurricane swept the nose of his plane up to gain height and then bailed out, but his parachute did not open and he plunged down into the sea in a "dead man's dive."

As the four ME 109s hurtled off to seek further victims, the crew of the lightship lowered their lifeboat and went to the place where the pilot had vanished, never expecting to see him again. Just as they were about to return to the lightship, the pilot broke surface, purple-faced and spluttering, "By God. Never thought I'd make it," he gasped to the lightshipmen, who pulled him jubilantly into the boat. "Went down like a stone and got stuck in the mud on the bottom."

One day seven Stukas flew over the North Goodwin and then commenced their devil's circus in the air, preparatory to diving into the attack. Only one Stuka came down in a shallow dive, and its bomb fell a few yards from the lightship's starboard bow. Bomb splinters whined and whistled everywhere. As the Stukas flew off, the crew of the lightship looked at each other in silence. Then one of them said, "I reckon that meant that they had not forgotten us and will be back some time."

In the meantime, the crew just carried on doing their job, listening to the news on the radio and fishing over the ship's side night and day to pass the time. The men of the North Goodwin accepted the fact that sooner or later they would be attacked and wished that they had guns aboard so that they could hit back.

One fine evening they watched a convoy of merchant ships coming round the South Foreland and into the Strait of Dover. As the lightshipmen stood watching, they heard the all-too-familiar roar of the engines of massed aircraft. Over a hundred German bombers were suddenly overhead, deluging everything in sight with high explosive. Over a thousand bombs must have fallen, some of them within a few yards of the North Goodwin and so close that the crew did not even remember hearing them explode.

When the air had cleared of smoke and water, one of the merchant ships was on her side and sinking fast. The lightshipmen again lowered their boat to search for survivors. They found only one and wished that they had not, for high pressure steam from a shattered steam pipe had cooked him alive. He died in the lifeboat, and for that the lightshipmen were grateful.

The fine, windless, cloudless days of later summer dragged on, and for the first time they could remember the crew of the North Goodwin longed for the clouds and rough seas of winter, which would help to hide them from the everlasting enemy aircraft. They no longer slept in their cabins below, for it was far safer to sleep in life jackets on the deck; that is, when one could sleep. Everyone's attention was now focused on watching and listening for the coming of German aircraft.

One morning a squadron of yellow nosed ME 109s roared at the lightship at wave-top level, and suddenly the

Relief crew leaving lightship tender to go aboard lightship in the dangerous Thames approaches

little red-painted lightship was the center of a storm of machine-gun and cannon fire, which whipped the sea up like a sudden squall. The lightshipmen hardly had time to fall flat before the attacking planes were gone, leaving the iron deckhouse and its teak doors full of bullet holes. By a miracle, the only casualty was a crewman, who had a long splinter of teak driven into his buttock like an arrow, much to the amusement of his shipmates.

The days passed by, and the lightshipmen kept watch, no longer horrified by the bodies of dead German and British airmen that floated back and forth on the tides until they sank.

One evening they stood watching 25 Dornier bombers, heavy with their bombloads, droning in towards the coast. As they flew over the land, they were met with such a storm of flak from the shore batteries that they turned back without dropping their bombs—straight for the North Goodwin lightship.

The crew just stood looking at each other. There was not the slightest sign of panic, for they had grown used to the idea that sooner or later this would happen. Even so, it was still hard to believe. Twenty-five heavy bombers to sink one small, unarmed lightship. It was like using a power hammer to smash an egg.

A junior crewman grabbed the arm of one of the older men. "Christ! Are that lot going to attack us?" he blurted in disbelieving tones.

The older man smiled grimly. "We won't have to wait long to find out, matey." As the Dorniers droned towards them at about 3,000 feet, the lightshipmen saw the doors of the bomb bays open; saw the bombs looking like small black dots floating gently down at first suddenly and hideously increase in speed and size.

"Down!" roared the skipper; and as the crew fell flat on the deck, blackness, flame, and thunder swallowed the tiny lightship; and black and stinking water deluged the prostrate crew.

The drone of the attacking bombers died into the distance, the smoke cleared, and the drenched lightship-men got to their feet and looked around with shocked, soot-streaked faces. They were still alive; nobody had even been hurt; and the lightship, except for the shattered glass of the lantern, was undamaged.

Long afterwards, one of that miraculously lucky crew learned from the District Officer of Coastguard, Ramsgate, that 150 bombs had been aimed at the North Goodwin and that the coast guards who had watched the attack were staggered when the lightship emerged still floating from the rolling smoke and waterspouts of the massed explosions.

As the lightship crew was examining their ship for damage, they heard the roar of combat planes. "Spitfires," somebody. "They'll deal with those bloody Dorniers." He was wrong, for the planes were a squadron of ME 109s, which poured a deadly swathe of cannon fire into a freighter that happened to be passing, opening up its side like an old tin can.

Then the German planes turned and roared straight over the lightship, but they did not fire. Instead, the German squadron leader saluted the lightshipmen as he flew over. One of them returned the salute—Winston Churchill's two-fingered gesture "V for victory."

One of the lightship crew, a big, hard-faced man from London's dockland, looked at the lightship master. "Don't ever ask me to pick up a "ditched" Jerry pilot again, skipper. They can bloody well sink for all I care."

Then they all went down to the master's cabin for a glass of rum. They felt that they deserved it.

At three o'clock in the darkness of the early morning, a trawler patrol boat from Dover moved quietly alongside the North Goodwin to evacuate the crew.

Down in the trawler's cabin, where they were cheered by more mugs of rum, the lightshipmen met an American war correspondent, who was immensely thrilled at being in the battle zone. "I'll spread the story of you lightshipmen clear across the States," he said in an admiring voice.

"Better make it snappy then," said the big crewman from London's dockland. "They call this place Hellfire Corner." He had hardly finished speaking when salvos from the German long-range guns began swishing overhead to fall on Dover. The youngest member of the lightship crew grinned at the others. "Shells or no shells," he said, "I'm getting my head down somewhere as soon as I get ashore. Don't remember how long it is since I had a proper sleep."

His sleep was a long one, for after the lightship crew had landed, he went off by himself and is believed to have walked right into the path of a falling shell. Whatever happened, he was never seen again.

In a preface to the author's book *Looming Lights*,* which describes some of the attacks by the Luftwaffe on English lightships, a total of 116 in all, the late Sir Geoffrey Callender, secretary to the National Maritime Museum, Greenwich, had this to say:

In this book the author describes from personal experience the atrocities committed against the lightships by the champions of the Crooked Cross. It is a formidable ar-

---

* Published in 1945 and reprinted in 1946 by Constable and Co. Ltd., 10 Orange Street, London, W.C. 2.

Trinity House lightship in the approaches to the Thames, removing and replacing navigational buoys damaged by fire from enemy aircraft.

raignment which no vindication can ever hope to con-
travene. It exposes one of the world's foulest crimes which
no tears of penitence can ever wash away, no apologies
ever condone.

For the first time since their inception nearly three
centuries ago, England's lightships had been attacked by
an enemy nation. Even the lighted buoys that marked the
seaways had been sunk by enemy aircraft. Now the battle
for the home seas was to be fought in darkness; the Nazi
E-boats, fast motor torpedo boats and gunboats, hunted
the British merchant convoys. The MGBs, MLs, and
MTBs (motor gunboats, motor launches, and motor
torpedo boats of the Royal Navy) hunted the E-boats.
And both sides hunted each other down the dark seaways
like rival wolf packs in fast, ferocious duels without quarter.
The MGBs, MLs, and MTBs of the Royal Naval Coastal
Forces have been aptly described as "The Spitfires of the
Sea," and the young men who manned these fast, formidable small ships were identical types to the young champions who flew Britain's Spitfires and Hurricanes. They
were young men from many walks of life and sections of
society with a common dedication—that of destroying the
sea power of the Nazis.

The little ships they fought in were divided into three
classes: The MTBs, whose function was to destroy enemy
merchant shipping wherever it might be found; the MGBs
for engaging the E-boats; and the MLs for a multitude of
tasks such as mine-laying, escorting convoys, and patrol and
rescue work. For this reason, the MLs were called the
"Maids of All Work" of the Royal Naval Coastal Forces.

Flotillas of these small ships with a big punch (armed
with torpedoes, Oerlikon 20-mm automatic cannon, 3-

pounder guns, .5 multiple Hispano heavy machine guns, and depth charges) operated from bases along the east coast of England from Lowestoft in Suffolk to Dover. Their names were frequently and aptly those of stinging insects, such as *Hornet, Wasp,* and *Midge.*

Opposing these high-speed, gasoline-driven craft were the high-speed, diesel-engined *Schnellboote* ("fast boats") of the Nazis. These were known to the British as E-boats, an abbreviation of "enemy war motorboats." In addition to these E-boats, the enemy had R-boats (Raumboote or sweepers), which were used for minesweeping and patrol work along the occupied coasts of France. The Nazi coastal forces also included destroyers, minesweepers and armed fishing trawlers.

In the battle for the home seas, the advantage lay with Germany, for the convoys of ships that carried food and war supplies to Britain were large and had comparatively few ships of the coastal forces to escort them. On the other hand, the enemy convoys were much smaller and had far greater numbers of ships of the German coastal forces to protect them.

The ships of the coastal forces of both sides had the hazards of the long-range guns, already described, to face. Both sides also had large minefields to protect their shipping routes and laid mines in each other's shipping lanes whenever they could.

In this little-publicized theater of the war, both the Germans and the British used their aircraft to advantage whenever targets presented themselves. So it was that the home seas around Britain were deadly dangerous at all times. And it was the British MTBs, MLs, and MGBs that helped the all-important convoys get through with food and supplies for the beleaguered island.

The battle for supremacy in the home seas of England was notable for the speed, ferocity, and gallantry of the innumerable actions that were fought. It was like a series of duels between teams of master swordsmen: thrust, parry, and disengage; thrust, parry, and disengage. But there were no seconds to see that there was fair play. And, like duels, these fast, ferocious, and highly specialized conflicts were frequently personal affairs between the combatants, who got to know each other's tactics.

On the late afternoon of Saturday, March 14, 1942, three fast MGBs of the 7th Flotilla, led by Lieutenant J. B. R. Horn aboard MGB 88, thundered out of Lowestoft Harbour into the deadly strip of sea off England's east coast called "E-boat Alley." The task of these three tiny warships, whose destructive power was out of all relation to their size, was a night patrol 20 miles off the coast of German-occupied Holland.

At 2200 hours, when the three MGBs were patrolling the bleak, black, heaving wastes of the unpredictable North Sea, they received a radio message from the East Coast Convoy Control that large numbers of E-boats were in their vicinity.

The British ships cruised all night, but saw nothing until gray dawn broke bitterly cold. In the cold, gray light the crews of the MGBs sighted the sharp bow wave of a large E-boat streaking at them at high speed. The enemy ship was almost as big as the three small MGBs put together and in the words of Lt. Horn, "Looked like an electric train."

The captain of the big E-boat must have known something of the reputation of the venomous little MGBs, however, for he altered course and departed at a speed estimated at 41 knots.

The three MGBs were even faster than this; and, like angry wild bees after a honey-stealing bear, they roared after the fleeing E-boat, bouncing like rubber balls over the looping, gray seas and hammering away at the E-boat with their 20-mm automatic cannon and multiple .5 machine guns.

To use the expression of British naval men, the big E-boat was "well and truly plastered" by the accurate fire of the three MGBs, and pieces were flying from her in all directions as cannon shells exploded and bullets struck home.

Lt. Horn's MGB 88 ran so close alongside the fleeing E-boat that her coxswain was able to empty his revolver at his counterpart aboard the enemy ship, which had been so badly hit that her hull was holed and she was already down by the bow. Some of the crew of the sinking E-boat jumped overboard, while others scrambled up on deck with their hands held high above their heads.

While the crews of the two of the MGBs were pulling gasping Germans from the bitterly cold water, the third MGB put a boarding party aboard the E-boat and the German first lieutenant was ordered to strike his ship's colors. He refused to do it; so the leader of the boarding party put him under armed guard, tore down the Nazi flag, and hoisted the white ensign of the Royal Navy in its place.

While this was happening, the crews of the MGBs suddenly sighted four more E-boats rushing at them, each one as big as the one they had defeated, and blasting away with all the guns they had.

The British MGBs, now short of ammunition, had to flee in their turn, leaving the damaged E-boat to be rescued by the others. As the MGBs broke off the action to retire at high speed, MGB 91 began to slow down, for its engine fuel pipe had been shattered by an exploding shell. The other two MGBs immediately laid a smoke screen round the disabled ship, whose first lieutenant manned the Oerlikon 20-mm cannon in place of the badly wounded gunner. He fired at the converging E-boats with such deadly accuracy that they sheered away, their shells and bullets cracking like whips round the intrepid lone gunner.

It seemed inevitable that the partly disabled MGB would be captured; but just as her crew were about to destroy the ship's papers and set fire to their ship, a thick, gray, wet North Sea fog suddenly descended and shut down visibility to nil.

Usually, sailors hate fog, but one of the crew of the damaged MGB said afterwards, "That was the first time in my life I've ever been glad of a fog at sea."

The two remaining MGBs were able to decoy the enemy away from the damaged MGB 91, which, with six of her crew of thirteen, including three officers, badly wounded, was at last able to limp safely back to Lowestoft Harbour. When the gunner of MGB 91 was being taken ashore, his arm nearly blown off by a shell, he was asked by the senior naval officer of the base how he was.

"Okay, sir," said the gunner. "We managed to get out of going to Sunday Shore Divisions, but we missed our tot of rum."

So the young men of Britain's coastal forces hid their courage and determination beneath a cloak of flippancy—young men who, like bullterriers, would fight anything regardless of its size and firepower. Nothing can illustrate this indomitable spirit better than the attack by five tiny MTBs and six long-obsolete Fairey Swordfish torpedo bombers on the battle cruisers *Scharnhorst* and *Gneisenau* and the heavy cruiser *Prinz Eugen*, guarded by a formidable escort of destroyers and massive air cover.

Of these three great warships, the *Scharnhorst*, known to the Nazis as "lucky *Scharnhorst*," was easily the most formidable. She was of 32,000 tons displacement, armed with 11-inch guns, and had oil-fired engines giving her a speed of 32 knots, enabling her to outstrip all other ships of her size. With a crew of 2,000 officers and men, she was launched at Wilhelmshaven in 1936, the first of Nazi Germany's new navy.

The fact that she was oil-fired and could thus be refueled at sea, vastly extended her lethal capabilities. She was able to prowl like a great gray wolf across vast distances of the sea—through the Baltic, along the coast of Norway, around Iceland and the Faroe Islands, and two-thirds of the way across the Atlantic Ocean towards America. In the course of her lone prowlings, the *Scharnhorst* had struck terrible blows at Britain. She had sunk the British aircraft carrier *Glorious*, with only 43 survivors of her crew of 1,032. *Scharnhorst* had also sunk the British destroyers *Ardent* and *Jocasta* and had annihilated the British armed merchant cruiser *Rawalpindi*, manned by Royal Naval pensioners and naval reservists, only 38 of whom survived.

In the meantime bombers of the RAF had kept the *Scharnhorst*, *Gneisenau*, and *Prinz Eugen* bottled up in Brest Harbour. The British navy was waiting for the day when those three great ships would try to escape, for it was essential that they should be destroyed.

At the beginning of February, 1942, intense enemy destroyer activity and minesweeping in the vicinity of Brest had alerted British Naval Intelligence, who, not dreaming that the three enemy warships would dare to attempt to escape to Wilhelmshaven by daylight, took no immediate action.

RAF Fighter Command at Biggin Hill also received information of unusual enemy naval activity off Dieppe and sent out a lone Spitfire to reconnoiter. The Spitfire's pilot radioed back to Biggin Hill, reporting what he had seen and then flew back to base, where the air controller took little notice of his report. He too must have thought that the great ships would not dare to run the gauntlet of the Strait of Dover in broad daylight. This assumption was one of the greatest blunders made by Britain during the war.

On February 11, 1942, the *Scharnhorst, Gneisenau,* and *Prinz Eugen,* with a powerful escort of destroyers, E-boats, and minesweepers and a swarm of ME 109s as air cover, left Brest Harbour and swept unhindered through the English Channel and the Bay of Seine. By midday that day the three warships were steaming through the Strait of Dover at 17 knots.

Six ancient Fairey Swordfish biplane torpedo bombers (known as string bags by RAF personnel) left Manston Airfield and flew in at 50 feet to attack the Nazi array. It was virtually a suicide mission, for the attackers were annihilated by a barrage of flak and the escorting ME 109s. Even the Germans admired the hopeless gallantry of the Fairey Swordfish crews, of whom only five out of eighteen survived. Lieutenant Commander Esmond, who led the doomed attack, received a posthumous Victoria Cross, Britain's highest award for gallantry. In the meantime, the long-range guns at Dover opened up on the three German warships, but were defeated by the foggy conditions that prevailed at the time.

At 1135 hours a message to the officer commanding coastal forces, Dover, reported that the three warships were steaming through the Strait of Dover. British MTBs which had just returned from exercise were instantly alerted, but only five were ready for action. At 1155 these five MTBs* thundered out of Dover Harbour into the windy, perilous Strait of Dover to confront a massive enemy array that only capital ships of the Royal Navy could have adequately dealt with. It was like five small weever stingfish darting out to attack a shoal of man-eating sharks.

Presently, the crews of the five small MTBs saw their objective; and it was a sight to daunt the bravest heart: three huge, graceful but lethal, gray ships, bristling with mighty guns, surrounded by a strong escort of destroyers, minesweepers, and, above, a swarm of ME 109 combat planes. On each flank of the warships there was also a whole division of E-boats, each boat faster and more heavily armed than the MTBs.

The crews of the five MTBs did everything they could to lure the E-boats away from the German battle cruisers, but to no purpose. The commanders of the five MTBs were now faced with the choice of firing their torpedoes at the German ships at long range and then escaping back to harbor at full speed or, in the ancient tradition of the British navy, "engage the enemy more closely" by smashing through the E-boat screen. This they did, and Lt. Commander Phumphrey, who led the tiny fleet of tiny ships, had to admit it was a desperate choice.

---

* No. 221 commanded by Lt. Commander Phumphrey; No. 219 commanded by Sublt. Mark Arnold Foster; No. 45 commanded by Lt. Hillary Gamble; No. 44 commanded by Sublt. R. F. Saunders, Royal Australian Naval Volunteer Reserve; and No. 48 commanded by Lt. C. A. Lew, Royal Canadian Naval Volunteer Reserve.

The five MTBs roared in at full speed until they were within a mere 200 yards of the E-boats, which immediately opened up a tremendous barrage of gunfire. Luckily, it was far too rough for accurate shooting; otherwise the MTBs would have been annihilated. As it was, they were able to fire their torpedoes at the German warships, but in the words of Lt. Commander Phumphrey, "with little hope of a hit."

The three big warships made a 90-degree turn three minutes after the torpedoes had been fired. The men aboard the MTBs saw a column of water leap up from the side of the *Prinz Eugen* and thought they had scored a hit. Afterwards it transpired that the *Prinz Eugen* had struck a mine that damaged her, but did not stop her.

By this time, the E-boats were laying a thick smoke screen round the three battle cruisers, and as the MTBs broke off the engagement and turned for home, they saw a German destroyer of the formidable Maas Class come shearing through the water straight at them. The MTBs, with their torpedoes gone, also "made smoke" and scattered into it at high speed.

As they went, two more British MTBs, No. 41 and No. 43, suddenly appeared. They too had fired their torpedoes without effect; nevertheless, they opened fire at the destroyer with their Oerlikon 20-mm cannon. The destroyer's captain, assuming that the two newcomers still carried their torpedoes, broke off the engagement and rejoined the main German fleet at high speed.

It was a gallant attack that failed, and the only consolation was that the crew of MTB No. 45 was able to rescue two of the pilots of the ill-fated Fairey Swordfish torpedo bombers.

When the German warships and their escort entered the North Sea, they were attacked again by British destroyers and bombers. And again the attack was a failure, for 15 British bombers were shot down, although both the *Gneisenau* and *Prinz Eugen* were damaged by floating mines. When the three German cruisers at last reached their home port of Wilhelmshaven, a great official celebration was held on the dockside.

Allowing the three powerful German warships to escape was a tremendous setback, for the fact that they were loose and on the prowl reawakened the fears of invasion in Britain. Until 1943, when the British battle fleet, led by Admiral Lord Fraser aboard H.M.S. *Duke of York*, reduced the *Scharnhorst* to a red-hot junk pile before sinking her off Norway, she destroyed a total of 100,000 tons of British shipping.

Three days after the three German warships had escaped, Singapore surrendered to the Japanese, and General Percival and 80,000 British and Commonwealth troops went into the barbarous prisoner-of-war camps of the Japanese. Winston Churchill described it as "the worst disaster and largest capitulation in British history." The whole of Britain and her allies were undoubtedly dismayed and humiliated by these two events. Nevertheless, the battle for the home seas was taking a turn for the better.

Although the *Scharnhorst, Gneisenau,* and *Prinz Eugen* had successfully escaped to Wilhelmshaven, the Germans had made a strategic blunder in abandoning Brest, for it was an important base from which British shipping in the Atlantic could be attacked.

During 1940 and 1941 the Luftwaffe had dominated the English Channel, the North Sea, and the vital Thames' approaches, but by 1942 British air power had increased sufficiently to counterbalance this threat, and British sea power dominated the home seas once more.

So it was in March 1942 that the Royal Naval Coastal Forces struck their greatest blow, the effect of which was to be felt far beyond the home seas. It was a combined operation with the RAF and commando units of the army in the daring, terribly costly, but nonetheless brilliantly successful, raid on St. Nazaire on the Atlantic coast of enemy-occupied France.

The chief purpose of this raid was to smash and render useless the only dock on the Atlantic coast capable of holding the 42,000-ton German battleship *Tirpitz*, then lying in Bergen and a major threat as a commerce raider. Secondary tasks were to render tidal, and thus useless, the pens of the U-boats, which were destroying British merchant ships, and to destroy the harbor installations of what was then a vital German naval base.

This historic assault on St. Nazaire, led by Colonel Charles Newman, who was later awarded the Victoria Cross and the croix de guerre, is brilliantly described in *The Battle of the Narrow Seas* by Lieutenant Commander Peter Scott, R.N. (Retired).

Over the entire war, the little ships of Britain's coastal forces fought 464 battles in the home seas, in which they destroyed 269 enemy ships for the loss of 76 of their own. These battles included the famous raid on Dieppe on August 19, 1942, where valuable information and experience were obtained for the Allied invasion of Europe on June 6, 1945.

But the greatest of these battles was the assault on St.

Nazaire, and of those who faced that hurricane of fire and death it can be truly written:

> If blood be the price of admiralty
> Lord God, we ha' bought it fair.*

* From "The Song of the Dead," in *The Seven Seas*, by Rudyard Kipling. Reprinted by permission of Mrs. George Bambridge, owner of the Kipling copyrights, and Methuen and Co.

14. Science at War

From the very beginning of man's history, it has been the most technically and scientifically advanced peoples who have dominated others both in peace and war.

The Beaker folk, who invaded Britain in 1900–1700 B.C., dominated the flint-using neolithic aboriginals by reason of their bronze daggers and superior bows and arrows.

The warlike dominance of the Biblical Hittites was due to a great degree to the fact that they used weapons of tempered iron while the majority of mankind was still using less durable bronze weapons and tools.

Archimedes, the Greek mathematician and inventor, is reputed to have destroyed the Roman fleet at the siege of Syracuse in 214 B.C. by means of mirrors that reflected and amplified the heat of the sun.

And it was the invention of radar that gave Britain the vital superiority in the air needed to win the Battle of Britain and thus save the country from invasion.

Robert (later Sir) Watson Watt, director of Britain's

Government Radio Research Station before and during the war, is the acknowledged inventor of radar, although a British inventor named Edward Appleton understood the principles of radar as early at 1924. Appleton, however, used his prototype equipment for atmospheric research, and it was A. F. Wilkins, an assistant of Watson Watt at the Government Radio Research Station, who demonstrated how the methods used by Appleton could also be used to detect aircraft at a distance. And the key to it all was a device called the cavity *magnetron*, which permitted the use of very short wave transmissions.

By 1940 at a Radio Research Establishment at Swanage, Dorsetshire, a team of British scientists assisted by men from Britain's universities, had already produced four vital radar devices, which helped the Allies win the war. These devices were known as AI, H2S, and OBOE, which had a later variant called G-H, and GEE.

AI, a variant of which was later developed by the Germans, was used by night fighter interceptor aircraft to locate their targets in the dark. In 1943 a radar device called *Serrate* was carried by British combat planes, enabling them to home on the AI transmissions of German aircraft and so seek out and destroy them. H2S was a radar device used by British Stirling, Halifax, and Lancaster bombers to locate and identify targets in the dark and was first used on January 30, 1943, to bomb Hamburg. The U.S.A. developed their own variant of this for use by the bombers of the U.S. Eighth Army Air Force, and it was known as H2X. To counter this, the Germans later developed *Naxos*, which homed on H2S transmissions.

OBOE, with its later improved version called *Album Leaf* and accurate within a radius of six miles, was a radar device used by the versatile Pathfinder Mosquito fighter-bombers. They were used for marking targets and could carry a 4,000-lb bomb to Berlin.

For pinpointing ground targets. OBOE was first used on December 20, 1942, when the German town of Lutterade was bombed. On March 5 and 6, 1943, OBOE-equipped aircraft of RAF Bomber Command devastated Essen, and on the night of June 24–25, this device enabled RAF bombers to destroy almost totally the difficult-to-locate town of Wuppertal-Elberfield.

GEE was a radar aid to navigation and target identication introduced in March, 1942, which did a great deal to boost the morale of bomber crews who hitherto had to fly "blind." It was used by bombers of the RAF to bomb Essen on March 8, 1942, and the Renault Works in German-occupied Paris on March 3, 1942.

As the war continued, many radar and antiradar devices were developed and used by both sides. ABC or *Airborne Cigar* was a device used to jam German combat plane control frequencies. *Aspirin* was used to jam the German *Knickebein* aircraft navigational aid. *Domino* was a device used to jam the German *X-Gerät* (X-system) bombing aid. *Mandrel* was the code name for the system used for swamping the German early warning radar system. *Meacon* was a device used to mask radio waves from German radio beacons, while RAF bombers carried a radar set called *Monica* to give them early warning of the approach of German night fighters.

Some of the code names given to the more elaborate uses of radar equipment were astonishingly unwarlike—*Musical Paramatta*, for example. This involved the ground marking of selected targets with colored target indicators dropped by Pathfinder Mosquito aircraft equipped with

OBOE. The targets thus marked would then be bombed by further waves of bombers. The sky marking of targets with colored markers dropped by OBOE-equipped Mosquitoes was code-named *Musical Wanganui*, while marking targets by means of flares or colored markers dropped by aircraft equipped with M2S radar was code-named *Newhaven*.

A device that brought havoc to the German radar defenses was code-named *Window* and was achieved by dropping myriads of strips of tinfoil from British aircraft. These strips showed up as a confusing mass on the German radar screens, which totally masked attacking bombers and fighters.

Window proved to be such a menace that Hermann Goering offered a tax-free award of 300,000 Reichsmarks to anyone who could invent a device to prevent the jamming or distinguish the difference between the tinfoil and the true targets. Such a device, which was attached to German radar equipment, was code-named *Goldhammer*, but apparently it had little effect, and at last the Germans retaliated with *Duppel*, their own version of *Window*.

As Germany began to catch up with Britain in radar techniques and development, one could almost say that the scientists and technologists of the opposing nations were fighting their own private war. Britain's radio experts developed *Tinsel*, code name for the radio transmission of engine noises broadcast on German night fighter control frequencies in order to confuse German pilots. The Germans went a step further and developed *Kurmak*, a code name for a transmitter that operated on British radar frequencies to transmit imitation radar signals to jam Allied radar-jamming devices. And so it went on.

From this mass of radio and radar equipment brought

into being by war came navigational aids to safety for aircraft and shipping, devices to probe and scan the ocean's
depths, and many other peaceful uses. After the war the
devices by which nations once hunted and destroyed each
other were at last used for the safety and well-being of
mankind.

At the commencement of the war, when German
scientists and technicians were lagging behind Britain in
the field of radar research and development, they were,
nevertheless leading the world in the field of infrared ray
(IR) techniques.

At the beginning of the war a number of British
scientists, including Professor F. M. Lindemann, the bitter
critic of Sir Henry Tizard, favored IR to radar; but fortunately for Britain, the latter soon proved its superiority.
As the war continued, the value of IR was recognized,
especially over short ranges, and a number of IR devices
were used by British and U.S. Infantry and tanks.

Germany, however, was largely the instigator of this
aspect of scientific warfare, and the number and variety of
IR devices Germans employed from the beginning of the
war showed a high degree of scientific and technological
skill. One of the first German substitutes for radar detection
equipment was an IR device known as *Adlergerät* or "eagle
equipment." This was an infrared telescope that could
detect aircraft by the heat emission from the engine exhaust
systems and that could also be used to lock searchlights
onto their targets.

Butterblume or "buttercup" was the delicate name
for a rather deadly piece of IR equipment. This was an
airborne device used for interception, but which was later
used by bomber and fighter aircraft as a means of locating

targets by heat emission, such as from power station and factory chimney stacks and the stacks of ships and locomotives.

Another ingenious form of intercept device of the IR type was known as *Falter*, meaning "folder," and was used to warn interceptor plane pilots that they too were being shadowed by IR equipment.

The great batteries of German coastal guns described in chapter 12 were also controlled by IR equipment code-named *Donau 60* or "Danube 60." The system was operated by four big parabolic mirrors stationed along the coast about five kilometers apart. These would detect passing ships by means of heat emission; transmit the bearing of the target to a central fire control station, which would correlate the data provided; and then transmit firing instructions to the batteries in the target area.

At the other end of the scale, IR devices could be used even for small targets. *Kater Gerät*, meaning "tomcat equipment," was an aptly named device used at night by German troops for detecting movement of their enemies. It looked just like a small telescope and was frequently used by night patrols. Equally small, but even more deadly, was the *Vampir ZG-1229*, an infrared night sight used by the Germans for their rifles.

The code name, which masked the deadliest weapon as yet conceived by man, was *Tube Alloys*, the name adopted by the Maud Subcommittee set up in 1940 to develop the atom bomb, when the nuclear research of Professor Peierls and Dr. Frisch of Birmingham University, England, had established the possibility of such a weapon.

A report to the president of the Secret Committee of the National Academy of Science, Washington, dated

November 6, 1941, read: "A fission bomb of superlatively destructive power will result from bringing quickly together a sufficient mass of the element U-235." It was the most doom-laden message ever written, and many notable scientists who realized the horrific effect the A-bomb would have were appalled at the thought of its use.

Sir James Chadwick, the greatest British nuclear scientist of his day, told two U.S. scientists that he wished he was able to say that the A-bomb would not work but he was almost certain that it would. Other eminent nuclear scientists, including Professor Max Bon of Edinburgh University, wanted nothing to do with the research and development of such a hideous weapon.

Professor Niels Bohr, the famous Danish nuclear expert, who helped in Britain and later in America with the development of the A-bomb and knew its awful potential, begged both President Roosevelt and Winston Churchill to ensure that the secrets of the A-bomb were internationally controlled. Winston Churchill, mistrusting the whole business, kept the secrets of the A-bomb to himself and the Conservative members of the national government. Britain, in the meantime, did not have sufficient labor, wealth, or development facilities for the production of the bomb; thus teams of British and U.S. scientists and technologists worked together on the deadly project in the U.S.

Germany, too, was carrying out nuclear experiments with heavy water, hoping to develop a fission bomb, and was deeply involved in a project that as yet the Allies had not considered—rocket research and development.

One of the first German rocket missiles, launched as early as 1940, was the 1,730-lb HS 293 glide bomb, which carried 550 kg of high explosive and was propelled by a rocket that burned for ten seconds after the missile had been launched. It failed in its first test, owing to steering control defects. These were quickly remedied and the glide bomb was put into operation with Dornier DO 217 bombers, which used it to attack Allied shipping, principally in the Bay of Biscay. The inherent weakness of the glide bomb lay in the fact that it was radio-controlled; its controls could easily be jammed by jamming transmissions. A number of variations of this weapon were developed, but it was finally abandoned.

Time was running out for the Third Reich, and numerous rocket projects had to be abandoned.

Nevertheless, work continued on two rocket projects that might well have snatched victory from the jaws of defeat for the Third Reich had the war not ended in 1945.

Development of the FZG-76, known to the Allies as the V-1, buzz bomb, flying bomb, and doodlebug, began at the Peenemünde Rocket Research Station in 1942, and it was successfully launched in December of that year.

The V-1 took the form of a midwing monoplane, with a length of about 25.5 feet and a wingspan of 17.5 feet. Its total weight on launching was 4,858 pounds, and fuel from a 150-gallon tank was forced by compressed air from cylindrical air bottles into an impulse duct engine mounted on the rear. Forward of the stubby wings and behind the chamber that carried an auto compass and other equipment was a warhead carrying 1,870 pounds of high explosive, of which two types were used, Fullung 52-A and the more powerful Trialen 105. The warhead was fused with three different types of fuses, electrical impact, mechanical impact, and clockwork delayed action, which ensured explosion however the missile eventually fell or landed.

At the beginning of the research on this formidable

weapon, fired from a concrete launching ramp, a piloted version was developed to determine flight performance and capabilities. This was done by removing the automatic controls and substituting a pilot's cockpit, together with ailerons, which were not fitted to the standard model. Testing these prototypes was a hazardous task, and at least one test pilot was killed, as were a number of launching personnel at the beginning when the V-1's mechanism failed on launching and the bomb exploded prematurely. The speed of the V-1 was well in excess of 400 m.p.h, which made it a difficult target for combat plane pilots to catch and destroy.

Mass production of this formidable terror weapon began in March, 1944; and during that year about 25,000 V-1s were produced, of which some 12,000 were ready for immediate launching. In spite of the fact that the Third Reich was tottering on the brink of defeat, production of the V-1 continued to mount. In March, 1945, 3,700 were produced, less than two months before the Montgomery's headquarters on Lüneburg Heath. The last V-1 was launched against England on March 29.

In all, a total of 9,251 V-1s were launched against England, and just under half of these were destroyed in the air by interceptor planes and antiaircraft batteries and by balloon barrages.

The V-1, the effect of which will be describe in Chapter 16, was more in the nature of a crude, pilotless jet plane rather than a true rocket. Nevertheless, German scientists had been at work for a long time on large rockets, with which they hoped to replace heavy artillery.

The rocket expert Wernher von Braun and General Dornberger began research and development work in the early 1930s on what was known as the A-series of rockets, work that culminated with the long-range rocket bombardment of England in 1944. The rockets of the A-series were liquid-fueled projectiles that originated at the artillery research station, Kummersdorf, although later research and development were carried out at Peenemünde research station. The first of the series, A-1, was not successful and was never launched but the A-2 rocket was launched successfully from the island of Borkum in the Baltic Sea five years before World War II commenced.

Rocket research and development at Peenemünde continued, and a rocket of the A-3 series was the first to maintain correct flight by means of a gyroscope. Only one was launched in 1938, and other launchings of the A-3 were failures. A-3 was now scrapped, and A-4, which had been on the drawing board since 1938, came into being, fueled with liquid oxygen and alcohol. Hitler called this his *Vergeltungswaffe*, meaning "vengeance weapon", better known as the V-2.

This formidable projectile weighed 13½ tons and, after launching, was directed onto a preset trajectory, the rocket motor being stopped at a predetermined point to allow the missile to fall on its target. Its accuracy was poor; for with a range of 180 miles it could only be directed onto a target 16 × 13 miles in area.

The "Vengeance Weapon" attack on England commenced on September 8, 1944, and ended on March 27, 1945, the last rocket falling in the county of Kent; in all, a total of 1,115 were launched.

Nor was the V-2 the only "Vengeance Weapon" that the Nazis had developed and intended to use on England. Even with defeat looming over them, the Nazis, aided by slave labor, had developed the V-3, which had the code name *High-pressure Pump* and which was called by those who worked on it the "England gun."

This was a series of mighty five-barreled guns, each barrel 416 feet long, which, firing from deep underground, was intended to continuously deluge London with 600 nine-foot-long projectiles every hour of the day and night. Fifty such underground batteries were intended to be sited along the Channel coast of France, and one such giant artillery complex actually did exist 350 feet underground at Mimoyecques near Calais.

In July, 1944, the site was attacked by RAF Lancaster bombers dropping 12,000-pound blockbuster bombs. Whether it was by incredible precision or incredible good luck will never be known, but one of these monster bombs hurtled straight into the gaping muzzle of one of the giant subterranean guns and so badly damaged the installations that the battery had to be abandoned.

British military experts who visited the site shortly afterwards said that the perpetual bombardment of London by such nightmare weapons would only have been a matter of time. Thereafter, Winston Churchill gave orders for the demolition of the site, and what was left of the wrecked "England gun" remains buried on the coast of northern France to this day.

15. Britain Emerges from the Shadows

APART FROM ADOLF HITLER, probably the most formidable "bogeyman" to haunt the British military leaders and public alike was Field Marshall Erwin Rommel, known as "the Desert Fox" because of his immense cunning and resourcefulness as a fighter. In the middle of February, 1941, Lieutenant General Rommel, as he was then, had defeated the British army under General Wavell, and he dominated the North African theater of war from then until El Alamein.

Such was Rommel's courage and military genius that the British and Commonwealth soldiers who fought against him, the British public, and even Winston Churchill were forced to admire the Desert Fox, who appeared like a ghost through the swirling desert sands with his men and tanks to wreak carnage in the British ranks. His continued victories not only dangerously lowered British morale at home, but endangered the position of Winston Churchill as Britain's war leader. Government ministers were saying among themselves that if General Rommel should finally be victorious in North Africa, it would be the end of Churchill.

It was then that a relatively unknown British lieutenant general named Bernard Montgomery emerged; a man who was to capture the imagination of the British public and the confidence and affection of the men he led and who later would become a field marshal and a viscount and one of the most brilliant, successful commanders in British history.

Later known as "Monty" to the men he led and to the British public, Lieutenant General Montgomery was like Rommel in some respects, for he had the same élan and the same humane concern for the lives of the men he led, but there the likeness ended. Where Rommel was a dashing, courageous, and inspired gambler, Montgomery was a cool, courageous, careful planner who was not to be driven into fighting a battle before he was ready. Not until he had the numbers of tanks, guns, and men he wanted would he open his offensive against the legendary Desert Fox.

When Montgomery was at last ready to strike, his tanks, guns, and men outnumbered those of Rommel by two to one, and the British had complete dominance in the air. The great battle, which started in the North African desert on October 23, 1942, was fought with ferocity and brilliance by both sides, with the British, in spite of their numerical superiority, losing more tanks than the Germans. But weight of numbers told at last, and on November 2, 1942, at the Battle of El Alamein, preceded by a British artillery barrage of unique ferocity and followed by equally fierce fighting on both sides, the seemingly unbreakable power of the Desert Fox was smashed.

At midnight on November 4, 1942, the BBC broadcast to the British people that Monty had defeated the Desert Fox and that Germany's hitherto invincible Afrika Korps was in full retreat.

The blitz-hammered, food-rationed British public, so inured to hardship and bad news, went wild with joy. Montgomery's triumph came to Britain like the news of Nelson's victory at Trafalgar, but without the sorrow of a great man's death in battle. Such was the rejoicing at the victory of El Alamein that, in spite of the fact that the ringing of church bells was to have been the signal for invasion, Winston Churchill ordered that the church bells should be rung for victory, although the bells were not rung until November 15, 1942. Britain was moving out of the shadows, but more darkness lay ahead before the war was won.

Whether the war itself was responsible or whether it "just happened" is debatable, but one of the most astonishing happenings in British social history was the emergence of the Beveridge Report for the planning of a peacetime welfare state at a time when Britain was locked in a global war.

Before the war the social security of the British public was indifferently catered for and poorly organized. About 16 million workers were eligible for financial aid if they became unemployed; about another 20 million were entitled to National Health Service sick pay if they became unemployed because of illness or accident, although their wives and children were not included in this scheme. Other sections of the working community—those who could afford it—privately insured themselves against unemployment owing to sickness and for medical and hospital charges by becoming members of various friendly societies and organizations such as the Ancient Order of Foresters, the Oddfellows, and Hospital Savings groups. People in the more highly paid jobs took out insurance policies against unemployment and sickness with various private insurance companies, but there was little or no social security for the lower paid workers and their families.

So it was that in February, 1941, the Trades Union Congress (TUC) sent members to the minister of health to stress to him the needs of the nation's workers in times of sickness and unemployment. Had the nation been at peace, the government might well have ignored this deputation; but as it was, the workers were important to the war effort and the government took action.

On June 10, 1941, a committee to look into the matter was appointed by Arthur Greenwood, minister without portfolio, whom Churchill had made responsible for the social welfare of Britain when the war was over. When one considers Britain's perilous position at this time, it was indeed an optimistic appointment.

The committee chosen by Arthur Greenwood consisted of 11 high-ranking civil servants, each representing the government departments responsible for various aspects of social welfare, and headed by Chairman Sir William Beveridge. For years Beveridge had been a social worker in the worst slums of London and knew better than any man the dire implications of unemployment and sickness and the poverty attendant on these social evils.

During World War I, Sir William had been a high ranking civil servant and before World War II was already director of the London School of Economics and recognized as Britain's leading sociologist. Such a combination of experience and qualifications soon bore fruit, and Sir William's proposals for a social welfare scheme for Britain were published in a 300-page report on December 1, 1942. The Beveridge Report, as it became known, aimed at welding all the nation's social security schemes into a coherent whole, which covered everything for the individual from birth to death, from maternity grants to funeral grants.

The postwar development of the welfare state was to have an unusual side effect. Workers and officials of various friendly societies, who previously had worked voluntarily or for a purely nominal sum now found themselves civil servants whose previous experience qualified them to deal with a host of social welfare problems in the new welfare state, which was to eliminate much poverty, disease, squalor, and misery.

The welfare state was to be achieved by cooperation between the state and the individual. While the state accepted the responsibility of organizing the social security, it expected the individual to provide for himself and his family to the best of his ability and not become a social parasite. Under the Beveridge Plan, family allowances would be paid for all children; the larger a family was, the more state benefit it would receive.

A National Health Service would be achieved by the state, the employer, and the employee, each contributing a fixed sum per week. It would ensure the individual against sickness and accident by providing sick payment and costs for hospitalization, doctors, and medicines. In time, these medical benefits became a party political issue in Britain, for, depending upon which political party was in power, drugs and medicines were sometimes free of charge while at other times they had to be paid for.

The Beveridge Plan set the national minimum income for every working man at £2 per week, a sum based on the assumed postwar value of the pound sterling.

Up to the time of the Beveridge Report, an unemployed man received 38 shillings a week from the state for 26 weeks. If he remained unemployed thereafter, his benefit expired, and he was forced to apply for National Assistance, which involved the grossly humiliating ordeal of "the means test," a bureaucratic probe into every penny and asset he owned and still bitterly remembered by many older Britons. Under the Beveridge Plan an unemployed man would receive 56 shillings a week for as long as he remained unemployed.

The national mood of euphoria at the thought of the utopia to come was somewhat dampened by the thought of the problem posed by the millions of old-age pensioners, for their tiny pensions, too, would have to be increased to maintain parity with the agreed minimum subsistence level. Even Sir William Beveridge himself agreed that dealing with this particular problem would prove so costly that it could not be adequately dealt with for another 20 years.

A point that aroused considerable criticism was that to achieve this welfare state, the cost of National Health and Unemployment contributions, borne jointly by the state, the employers, and the employees, would inevitably increase. History has proved that these fears were more than justified, for the costs of these contributions have risen periodically ever since.

Sir William Beveridge remained undeterred, however, for he felt that the workers would be encouraged to do their utmost to help win the war as soon as possible, with the promise of social security awaiting them once the war was won. Postwar Britons would be progressing towards "the world fit for heroes to live in," which their fathers of World War I were so glibly promised but never saw materialize.

In spite of his practical plans for a brave new postwar world, Sir William Beveridge had his detractors. Be that as it may, he was not to be deterred and energetically demanded that the government should implement his plan and that a new Ministry of Social Security should immediately be formed to commence the massive and complex task of organizing the welfare state.

The right wing members of the Tory (Conservative) party, who by no stretch of the imagination could ever be accused of sympathy towards the working classes, were quick to decry both Beveridge and his plan, saying, among other things, that the increased unemployment benefit would make thousands of people work-shy and idle, preferring to live "on the dole" at the nation's expense. Less extreme Tories were not so outspoken, but said, in effect, that while the plan seemed a good one, only the peacetime trade figures would show whether it was practical.

As might be expected, the Labour party approved the Beveridge Plan, as did the Liberal party and the general public. Winston Churchill, on the other hand, appears to have been thoroughly irritated by this planning of a welfare state. This dream of a peacetime utopia was to him an irrelevancy that contributed nothing towards the winning of the war. With his razor-keen perception, he undoubtedly realized that this plan would prove to be a mighty weapon for the Socialists in times of peace—as indeed it proved to be, for it contributed considerably to the landslide victory of the Socialists in the first election after the war. And Churchill, though he had changed his political allegiance in times past, had never been a Socialist.

After considerable debate and argument in the House of Commons, members of the Cabinet agreed to 16 of Sir William Beveridge's 23 recommendations, but only in principle. As the debating and the arguing about the proposed welfare state and its innumerable aspects and implications continue, the working classes of Britain perceived one thing very clearly. The gulf between themselves and the Tories was as wide and as deep as it had ever been. This, too, contributed to the massive Socialist victory in the first postwar general election.

In the meantime, the British public wanted to hear something positive about the proposed welfare state, which they felt would compensate them for the miseries they had endured and were yet to endure. Thus on March 1, 1943, Winston Churchill, still irritated by the whole thing, broadcast to the nation. He said that he visualized that the present coalition government or a national government would continue after the war and would implement his Four-Year Plan, which was based on the Beveridge Report, although he did not say as much.

The Four-Year Plan included compulsory national insurance, which would cover everybody from birth to death. A National Health Service would provide doctors, hospitals, drugs, and medicine for all. A massive building program would be implemented to replace houses destroyed by bombing; slum dwellings would be demolished and modern houses erected in their place. Agriculture would be subsidized to provide cheap food at stable prices; in time, industry would be nationalized, and there would be no more unemployment. Even for such a prodigy as Winston Churchill, it was flying in the face of providence to make such an utterance as the latter.

In the meantime, other plans were afoot for Britain and America. The Allies were planning the greatest sea and land assault in history to deliver a devastating thrust at the black heart of the Third Reich. Germany was planning, too, to bring yet more death and destruction to England by means of new and terrifying weapons.

16. The Last Days of the War and Germany's Defeat

THE CIVILIAN POPULATION of Britain had endured hell on earth during the blitz of 1940 and had suffered sporadic air raids from that time onwards. However, the terrible attacks by massed fleets of bombers seemed to have become a thing of the past, and the British public was hoping against hope that they would never come again.

It was a vain hope, rudely dispelled towards the end of January, 1944, when German bombers again attacked in force, showering thousands of incendiary bombs and much heavier and more destructive high-explosive bombs on London, Bristol, and Hull and towns in South Wales. Moreover, the civilian populations of these places had an additional ordeal to endure—the terrifying, deafening hiss and roar of the multiple antiaircraft rocket batteries used to "box-in" the German bombers.

This new weapon, which filled the skies with fiery cubes of death and destruction, added to the hellish din and confusion. The sound of the rockets swishing upwards, hundreds at a time, sounded almost exactly like a deluge of bombs swishing downwards.

Every time these hydra-headed monsters blasted skywards, everybody dived for cover, until they learned to recognize the sound. In the meantime, the double effect of the upward-hurtling rockets and the downward-hurtling bombs made existence even less endurable than in the early days of the blitz—if such a thing were possible.

Between the end of January and the middle of April, 1944, the Luftwaffe hit Britain with short, lightning-swift, but devastating attacks. During February nearly a thousand Londoners were killed, thousands of houses in southeast London were destroyed, and a number of major conflagrations raged in the London area. Even so, this destruction was as nothing to the awful retribution that RAF Bomber Command and the U.S. Eighth Army Air Force based in Britain were meting out to the towns and cities of Nazi Germany.

At this time, there was a growing atmosphere of tension and excitement in Britain.

In the spring of 1944, endless streams of tanks, guns, and military vehicles of every kind choked the roads to the south coast. The bomb-battered port of Southampton was suddenly crammed with shipping and hundreds of unusual-looking craft. Houses and buildings in the vicinity were taken over by the military, and speculation was rife.

Seamen aboard ships anchored in the lower reaches of the River Thames, now crowded with hundreds of tank-landing craft, saw numbers of huge and unwieldy steel and concrete caissons being towed downriver. The watchers did not know then that these were sections of the prefabricated Mulberry Harbours, which were to be towed across the

Channel to provide floating havens and landing places for the Allied invasion of Europe.

The men on the anchored ships also speculated as to the purpose of the little red lightships with *Juno* and *Kansas* painted in large white letters on their sides. These small ships, once used to mark the perilous places of the sea, were soon to mark places infinitely more perilous—the invasion beachheads on the coast of France.

Britain was suddenly full of vast and mysterious movement, and every railway depot and siding on the south coast was crammed with war vehicles, stores, guns, and ammunition.

In the meantime, the crews of the German reconnaissance aircraft prying over England flew back with reports and photographs of obvious invasion preparations along the creeks and on the hitherto deserted airfields of the Kent and Essex coasts. The German reconnaissance crews did not know that they were the victims of a gigantic hoax. The photographs that RAF Fighter Command had so obligingly allowed them to take were pictures of full-size dummy landing craft and gliders of plywood and full-size rubber "tanks," which were blown up like balloons.

The true objectives of the German reconnaissance aircraft, thousand upon thousand of tanks, guns, war vehicles, and mountains of war supplies and ammunition, were shrouded carefully beneath the huge trees in the eerie vastness of the New Forest, which despite its name, has existed for more than a thousand years. In addition, the skies above thundered to the passing of great fleets of British and American aircraft—fleets such as the world had never seen before and hopefully, we trust, will never see again.

In southern England hundreds of thousands of Allied troops were waiting tensely, confined to their camps and forbidden contact with the outside world.

In the meantime, bomb-battered Germany, still ferociously implacable, was also making preparations.

All along the desolate Pas de Calais area of France, stark, towering structures of steel and concrete were rearing skywards, looking like grim travesties of the roller coasters seen in amusement parks. Few people knew then what their function was, but they were soon to learn, and to their cost. Since as early as 1943, Allied intelligence agents had warned the British government that Germany was preparing some form of long-range bombardment of England, and Winston Churchill had already warned the British public that it would be subjected to some new form of enemy attack.

In the meantime the D-Day invasion of German-occupied Europe, which should have commenced on June 5, 1944, was delayed by gales and high seas until the early morning of June 6. Never before in the history of mankind were there such a mighty armada of ships seen on the high seas and such giant fleets of aircraft rocking the air with the continuous thunder of their passing.

The invasion was preceded by one of the most awesome and yet somehow inspiring sights ever accorded to mankind. The great capital ships of the Royal and U.S. navies, lined in gray, massive array, giant guns jutting skywards, wreathed in great, billowing gusts of smoke and flame, filled the air with man-made thunder as they poured a hurricane of destruction on the enemy gun positions. Equally awesome, but in a different way, were the ungainly rocket ships with their tier upon tier of rockets, which hissed endlessly up, raking the skies like fiery claws and obliterating everything where they fell in huge bursts of smoke and flame.

The Americans were the first to land, followed an hour later by the British. Despite the naval bombardment that preceded the landings, the fighting was ferocious and without quarter. Small wonder, for the German troops were led by their hero the Desert Fox, who despite his defeat at El Alamein, remained undaunted to the day of his death so near at hand.

When darkness fell to shroud the carnage of D day, 156,000 British, American, and Allied troops had landed on the enemy beaches.

"We'll be back, you Jerry bastards," the battered but unbroken men of Dunkirk had once shouted, and now they were back, and this time they were not alone.

By the end of that historic month something like 900,000 fighting men and 150,000 war vehicles were in France, and by July 9 Field Marshal Montgomery's forces had driven the Germans out of Caen and occupied the town. The Americans, who had been pinned down by massive enemy pressure to the west of Caen, smashed through on July 25 and swept through France as the German panzers had done four years before.

Even though they were hemmed in by the Allies to the west and by the swiftly advancing Russians to the east, the Germans still had the will and the means to wreak deadly havoc on English civilians.

About the middle of August, 1944, an old duck shooter hunting in the marshlands of Kent looked up at the sky and listened, prepared to fall flat on his face if he saw what he thought he heard. From away to the east over the gray sea came a strange, menacing sound, swiftly increasing to a noise like the stuttering roar of a giant blowtorch. Crouching in the long grass, the old duck hunter watched with a puzzled expression as the strange aircraft, trailing a long tail of yellow flame, streaked overhead. "Looks like one o' they danged German fighters on fire," he mumbled to himself, and even as he spoke, the menacing sound ceased, and the flying object streaked downwards. Seconds later, there was a huge, yellow red flash of flame and a shock wave like the edge of a jagged blade slashed momentarily across the clear sky, followed by the rumble of a heavy explosion.

The old man picked up his shotgun and got to his feet. "Well, one thing's fer sure," he grunted. "That warn't no onery fighter plane, less'n it wus carrying a big owd bomb." He was half right, for although the flying object was not a fighter plane, it *was* carrying "a big owd bomb." It was one of the first of the flying bombs, or V-1s, launched from the steel and concrete ramps in the Pas de Calais. Its hideous appearance, terrifying sound, and unpredictable flight, plus the fact that it was launched blindly against civilians, made the flying bomb a classic terror weapon.

A few days after the first flying bombs had been seen roaring and stuttering in from the sea over the Kent and Sussex coasts, a sustained bombardment by the new weapon began and reached a peak of about 100 a day, although to the people who endured the ordeal it seemed like a thousand. On August 15 the air raid sirens in the London area sounded about midday to warn of the new onslaught, and the all clear sirens did not sound until late the same evening.

The Londoners, inured to bombing, did not panic,

but they were shocked and frightened nonetheless, for this attack seemed endless. It was like standing helplessly in the path of a demented giant who was endlessly hurling monstrous flaming darts at random.

Sometimes the flying bombs were trapped in the wires of barrage balloons or exploded in the air by flak, seeming to blossom in the sky like some monstrous, red gold bloom. Only the latest, fastest interceptor planes could catch these 400-m.p.h.-plus horrors, and even then the pilots had to be very careful how they dealt with them. They could not be shot down over towns and villages, only over the sea, the marshes, fields, or downs. Moreover, if they were blown up in the air, they were liable to annihilate the plane and pilot.

Eventually, some daring pilots perfected a technique that was breathtaking to watch and that will never be forgotten by those who saw it. With incredible skill and tremendous courage, the pilots would maneuver their planes alongside the roaring, deadly brute and sliding the wing tip carefully beneath the wing tip of the flying bomb, would tilt it so that it flew back out to sea, sometimes to explode on enemy-held territory.

The American servicemen in Britain called the flying bombs "doodlebugs" because they behaved as unpredictably as those erratically flying insects. Never was a name more apt, for one never knew what a flying bomb might do. Generally, the engine would cut out when the fuel was exhausted; then the bomb might glide for miles before it hit and exploded. Sometimes it would drop like a stone and at other times spiral earthwards like a shot-down plane. Sometimes these bombs would crash down with their engines still roaring. At other times and for no known reason, they would stand up on their tails, climb dement-edly into the sky, stall, and crash straight back to earth. Then again they might, with or without the engine running, start jinking and weaving like a frightened snipe before they finally crashed and exploded.

It was this terrifying unpredictability that unnerved most people. Some folk even said that doodlebugs had a homing device that enabled them to home on single individuals and chase them. Thus was born a legend, which though only nonsense, did seem to have some foundation of truth to those who endured the nerve-racking experience of being "chased."

During the flying bomb attack on England, the author, having landed from a ship anchored in the lower Thames, was walking through the marshes to the town of Gravesend, further upriver. Several flying bombs were roaring over at the time, and suddenly one of them seemed to single out the author for attention. So real was the illusion that he started to run, which was very silly anyway. Lower and lower came the stuttering, roaring doodlebug. When the author turned right, *it* turned right; when he turned left, *it* turned left. Finally, he fell flat on his face in a very dirty part of the marsh, where cattle had been grazing, while the bomb roared overhead, finally to fall in the marshes and explode harmlessly.

Another unnerving thing about the flying bomb was that sometimes you could see one, but not hear it, and at other times you could hear one, but not see it. In the first instance, it usually meant that the engine of the bomb had shut off, and it was about to fall. In the second instance, it meant that it was so low that you could not see it anyway and was thus far too close for safety.

The author was standing outside his flat one night at Sutton on the outskirts of south London, watching the doodlebugs flame over. The sensible thing would have been to huddle in an air raid shelter. Nevertheless, there was an unholy fascination about these fiery oriflammes trailing across the sky that bred near-suicidal curiosity.

Suddenly, a horrible stuttering roar seemed to engulf the unwise watcher; and before he even had time to fall flat, a doodlebug only just cleared the tops of some nearby house chimneys, passing so close that one could feel the hellish heat of the crude jet engine and smell the stench of burning fuel. It fell and exploded only two streets away, demolishing many houses and killing a number of people.

Quite apart from its undeniable psychological effects as a terror weapon, the flying bomb was far more deadly than any conventional bomb of the same explosive power. Where the conventional bomb not infrequently buried itself before exploding and thus mitigated its blast effect to some degree, the flying bomb exploded on the surface, and the blast of its 1,870 pounds of high explosive was horrific. Buildings and houses were swept away like chaff; people near the blast were atomized, and those further off were sliced piecemeal by flying glass and debris.

In the case of raids by bomber aircraft, people could get to shelter and stay there until the all clear sirens sounded, but the seemingly endless procession of flying bombs made this almost impossible, so that people just went about their business in many cases and hoped for the best in a fatalistic manner.

Something like 7,000 flying bombs, also called buzz bombs, were launched against England; and although more than half of them were destroyed in the air, their toll was a brutal one. About 5,500 people were killed and another 16,000 severely injured, with 25,000 houses in London and its suburbs totally destroyed or wrecked beyond repair.

London, as usual, took the weight of the attack, and the most terrible incident of the entire bombardment occurred when a flying bomb hit the chapel of the Regiment of Guards during divine service. One hundred and nineteen people died, and one hundred and two were badly injured; among the casualties were many well-known officers with distinguished records.

Allied bombers dropped nearly 150,000 tons of bombs on the flying bomb launching sites, but only when Field Marshal Montgomery at the head of the British Second Army captured many of the launching sites in late August, 1944, did the flying bomb menace diminish. It did not cease completely until after the British and American forces had crossed the River Rhine in late March, 1945. By that time, flying bombs, now ranging further afield, had killed 27 people in the town of Oldham, Lancashire.

In the meantime, yet another form of death and destruction was hurtling down from the English skies.

On September 8, 1944, a few weeks after the French people and French resistance fighters had liberated Paris from the domination of the Nazis, Londoners saw a blinding white flash over Chiswick, followed by a heavy explosion and, seconds later, a cyclonic roar from the sky. The first of the V-2 rockets, Hitler's "Vengeance Weapon," had fallen. So fast did it come that its explosion outstripped the rushing roar of its descent.

As the V-2s continued to fall at the rate of about five or six a day, cautious officialdom declared that the explosions were due to defective gas mains. Bomb-battered Britons grinned knowingly at this clumsy, if not downright insulting, subterfuge and thereafter referred sarcastically to the V-2s as "flying gas mains."

Terrifying though the V-2 rockets were, they were less effective as a terror weapon than the flying bomb, and the British public treated them with fatalistic sangfroid. They said, in effect, that the rockets came so fast and so unexpectedly that there was nothing you could do about them anyway. If a rocket "had your name on it," it was just too bad and that was that. A new phrase was coined, "getting a rocket," which generally meant receiving a severe reprimand from a superior when you least expected it.

On clear days people used to stand and watch the vapor trails of the rockets as they arched through the sky, giving a resounding cheer when the 13½-ton missile exploded prematurely, as it sometimes did, owing to heat caused by friction as it descended into the atmosphere.

"The Nazis are beaten. This is their last fling," seemed to be the general opinion, but before the V-2 bombardment ceased, about the same time as the cessation of the flying bombs, 500 to 600 rockets had fallen on England, most of them on battered London, killing nearly 3,000 people and badly injuring more than 6,000.

Hardly had the V-1 and V-2 bombardment ceased when the British people suffered another grievous blow, this time to their hearts and spirits. On April 12, 1945, President Roosevelt died.

Winston Churchill was deeply affected, for a close relationship had existed between the two leaders. Even before they met for the first time, 1,800 letters had passed beween them, and their first meeting was portentous and dramatic. Churchill had crossed the Atlantic on Britain's latest battleship, H.M.S. *Prince of Wales*, which steered a zigzag course at high speed and maintained strict radio silence to evade enemy submarines.

In August, 1941, in Placentia Bay, Newfoundland, the H.M.S. *Prince of Wales* anchored close to President Roosevelt's cruiser, U.S.S. *Augusta*. In this manner, the two great men met for the first time, and the outcome of this meeting was the signing of the Atlantic Charter and the cementing of the Anglo-American alliance. Thereafter, Churchill and Roosevelt met many times—at Washington, D.C., Quebec, Cairo, Casablanca, Teheran, and Yalta. Churchill's admiration and affection for President Roosevelt was profound, for he called the president "the greatest American friend we have ever known." When the president died, the British nation felt grief and shock. For in spite of Roosevelt's frail health, he had emanated a granite strength of will and purpose, and his humanity had shone like a beacon during five years of unprecedented inhumanity.

This inhumanity was made shockingly manifest when the Allied troops saw for the first time the horrors of the Belsen, Buchenwald, and Dachau concentration and extermination camps of the Nazis. The shock and nausea of the Allied troops at what the camps revealed swiftly turned to cold fury, and after forcing the S.S. guards of the camps to bury many of the victims, they thrust forward like a sword from the west, while the Russians swept in from the east.

The Germans fought with traditional fury and fanaticism in the north, around Berlin, in the south, and facing the advancing Russians to the east. But now the Nazis were learning the bitter meaning of the word they had once proudly coined—*Blitzkreig*, or "lightning war." On April 25 the American forces met the Russians at the River Elbe, while Field Marshal Montgomery's army swept triumphantly to the shores of the Baltic Sea.

Thus was the once proud and mighty Third Reich cleft asunder.

On April 30 two days after Italian partisans had executed the defeated Mussolini and his mistress, and with Berlin hemmed in by Russian tanks, Adolf Hitler, hiding in his private bunker in the shattered Berlin chancellery, first poisoned his mistress, Eva Braun, and then shot himself dead.

On May 1, 1945, Grand Admiral Karl Doenitz broadcast to the defeated German nation that Hitler had died "a hero's death in the capital of the German Reich, having led an unmistakably straight and steady life." It was a pathetic utterance, for although Hitler had always been obsessed with the gloomy, tragic grandeur of Wagner's Nordic operas, in death he was no Siegfried.

Three days later, on Lüneburg Heath, the representatives of Admiral Doenitz tearfully surrendered the bulk of the German forces to Field Marshal Montgomery. The document of surrender was signed on a trestle table covered with army blanket, and Monty's only sentiment appears to have been irritation at the loss of the pen with which the document was signed. "I suppose somebody pinched [stole] it," he said testily.

On May 7, 1945, at Rheims, the final document for the unconditional surrender of Germany was signed. After signing it, General Jodl said, "With this signature the German people and the German armed forces are, for better or worse, delivered into the victor's hands."

That same day, General Eisenhower, supreme commander in Europe, sent the following message to the Combined Allied Chiefs of Staff: "The mission of this Allied Force was fulfilled at 3:30 A.M., local time, 7 May 1945. Eisenhower."

The next day at 3:00 P.M., after a special lunch for Chiefs of Staff at No. 10 Downing Street, Winston Churchill broadcast to the jubilant British nation:

Our gratitude to our splendid Allies goes forth from all our hearts in this island and throughout the British Empire. We may allow ourselves a brief period of rejoicing but let us not forget for a moment the toil and efforts that lie ahead.

The first task amid that toil and effort was the overthrow of as yet undefeated and unrepentant Japan. In the meantime, the next day a national holiday was declared and was marked by the unique spectacle of the traditionally reserved British people rejoicing with all the abandon and spontaneous gaiety of a Mexican fiesta. All the shops were shut; strings of colored flags hung across the streets; whole forests of Union Jacks jutted from windows and buildings and from the grubby hands of small children. Wildly cheering crowds pushed Winston Churchill's car all the way from Downing Street to the House of Commons. When he entered the House, members sprang to their feet, cheering as wildly and enthusiastically as the crowds outside; and after Churchill had addressed the members, he moved that all should go to St. Margaret's Church, Westminster, to give thanks to God for victory and deliverance from the enemy. St. Paul's Cathedral was also packed with people giving thanks for victory and deliverance.

That evening at six o'clock Winston Churchill addressed a mighty throng of cheering, shouting, flag-waving people from a balcony in Whitehall. "This is your victory," he told them. "It is the victory of the cause of freedom in every land. In all our long history we have never seen a greater day than this."

King George VI allowed his daughters, Princess Elizabeth, Britain's queen today, and her sister, Princess Margaret, to mingle with the merrymaking throng outside Buckingham Palace. All public places and statues were floodlit, and searchlights laced joyously across the sky, vying with rockets and exploding fireworks. Stocks of liquor, kept for the occasion, appeared everywhere. People drank, danced, sang, played jazz music in the streets, kissed each other and kissed strangers. Some even fired guns in the air, something that under normal circumstances would have earned them a jail sentence. The great fountains of Trafalgar Square were filled with drenched, ecstatic people sporting like joyous sea lions.

Every town, city, village, and hamlet in Britain threw open its doors and its arms. Long tables were set up in the streets, and the children were seated to eat things they had only heard of but never seen, jellies, custards, trifles, cakes, and jams.

Church bells, once to be the signal for invasion, rocked the air the length and breadth of Britain. Great bonfires flamed from hilltops and high places up and down the kingdom, as they had done five centuries before to warn of the approach of the Spanish Armada.

On this day the British people went wild with joy, for the dread shadow of the swastika no longer lay across the land.

17. Churchill's Defeat at the Polls and Japan's Surrender

As ALREADY STATED, Winston Churchill could never be regarded as a party politician, for he hated and despised the maneuvering for position, the strife, and the bitterness of party politics, which conventional politicians accept as part of the political scene.

At the end of the war, he struggled hard to keep this atmosphere out of politics and to keep the national government together. Strangely enough, it was two dedicated Labour party members, Clement Attlee, soon to be prime minister, and Ernest Bevin, who supported him in this lost endeavor. But the rest of the Labour and Conservative members did not want this; they wanted to be back in the bearpit of peacetime party politics.

So it was that on May 23, 1945, the national government was dissolved, with the promise to the nation of a general election to be held on July 5. Winston Churchill, in the meantime, tried to establish a peacetime national government representing all political parties and even included in this caretaker government, as it became known, new ministers who in the past had been bitterly critical of Churchill and the coalition government. This caretaker government only lasted for two months, but it is memorable for the fact that it introduced the Family Allowance Bill, which was a step towards the long-planned welfare state.

In the meantime, the various political parties of Britain were organizing their campaigns for the general election so soon to come, and Winston Churchill's own campaign was possibly one of the most disastrous aspects of his political career. Everything was against him from the beginning. He was getting old and was desperately tired, for the burden he had carried for more than five years would have broken most men and sent them to any early grave.

Even though the war with Germany and Italy had been won and Japan was tottering on the verge of cataclysmic defeat, Churchill was distracted by matters that to him were more important and direful than the outcome of any general election. The war had drained Britain of her once fabulous wealth and resources; millions of British citizens had died; the British Empire was already crumbling; and the imponderable menace of Stalinist Russia now loomed as large as, and even larger than, the Nazi menace had once loomed.

Churchill had already written to Stalin, telling him bluntly that there was little comfort in looking into a future where the Communists and the Western World faced each other in a quarrel that could tear the world apart. Moreover, in a letter to President Truman, Churchill wrote despairingly of the iron curtain that had dropped down on the front in Europe.

Small wonder that Churchill could not give his mind to the approaching general election. To make matters worse, he had powerful political foes, not only in the Labour party, but also in the Conservative party, a number of whose members still regarded him as an untrustworthy Conservative.

The general tone of Churchill's electioneering speeches at this time was so bitter, confused, and lacking in constructive ideas that some sections of the national daily press declared frankly that he was tired and worn out and should retire while he still had the respect of the British people.

As one looks at events in retrospect it might have been better if Winston had retired with dignity at this time, but it was not his way to walk away from any battle, physical or political. Moreover, nothing in the world could have robbed him of the respect, admiration, and affection not only of the British, but of the Americans also.

Probably beyond any Briton who ever lived, Winston Churchill was a man of mighty vision, and perhaps his mightiest vision of all was that of Britain and America united in common citizenship: Britons and Americans with common passports, united by "the gift of a common mother tongue" and moving freely in each other's countries. But the war-weary British had no such splendid dreams; all they were concerned with was the immediate future in which, from their point of view, Churchill had no longer any part to play.

Towards the end of his electioneering campaign, Winston went on a railroad tour of Britain, and wherever his train stopped, the thronging people cheered him wildly and enthusiastically. But they were cheering a great warlord, who had saved them from annihilation and had led them forward on the path of victory, not a man who hoped to lead them back along the tortuous, hazardous roads of peace.

Many and varied reasons have been presented as to

the rejection of Winston Churchill as a peacetime leader by the British public, and perhaps the real reason is that the public knew instinctively that few war leaders, however great, had served their countries well in times of peace.

This thought may have been in Churchill's mind when, during a luncheon party at No. 10 Downing Street, he asked General Slim of Burma how he thought his soldiers would vote. When Slim said uncompromisingly that 90 percent of them would vote Labour, Churchill asked how the other 10 percent would vote. When Slim said that they would not vote at all, Churchill surely must have seen the writing on the wall.

It was characteristic of Britain's Grand Old Man that on the day when the results of the general election were being declared, he sat in his grim "war room" beneath Storey's Gate, listening to the results of the new battle he was fighting and clad in his zipper-fronted "siren suit," which had so intrigued and delighted America by its novelty and simplicity.

The Labour party swept to victory in the greatest political landslide in British history, and when Lord Moran spoke sympathetically to Winson about the ingratitude of the British people, Churchill just said quietly, "I wouldn't call it that. They have had a very bad time. I'm not certain that the Conservative party could have dealt with the labor troubles that are coming."

At six o'clock that evening he left his "war room," never to return again and went to Buckingham Palace to tender his resignation as prime minister to King George VI.

King George the Good, as he is affectionately called in modern British history, was as sad at Winston Churchill's fall from office as he was at Neville Chamberlain's and also told the ex-prime minister that he thought the people were very ungrateful after the way Winston had led them during the war. Churchill just said that with the massive majority the Labour party now had and with careful management, they would remain in power for years to come. The king then asked Churchill if he should send for Clement Attlee to form the new Labour Government, and to this Churchill, now leader of the opposition, agreed.

After the king had seen Clement Attlee and asked him to form the new government, he wrote a moving letter to Churchill, saying that his great vision and grasp of essential matters had been a great comfort to him, the king, during the dark days of the war and that his conduct as prime minister and minister of defense had never been surpassed.

America was stunned at Britain's rejection of her great war leader, but *The New York Times* of July 27, 1945. accurately assessed the reason for the rejection of Churchill and his coalition government, saying, "It is perhaps the natural reaction of a nation sick of war and the symbols of war and moved above every other impulse by a desire for change."

On August 6, 1945, the BBC announced to the British people that the first A-bomb had been dropped by the United States on Hiroshima, Japan. Three days later another was dropped on Nagasaki. In these two small but devasting sunbursts the project masked by the mundane code name of *Tube Alloys* came to its cosmic completion.

As the dread effects of the new weapon became known, people were shocked and horrified, saying that such a monstrously evil thing should never have been unleashed

against mankind. However, in his first speech in the House
of Commons as leader of the opposition on August 7, 1945,
Winston Churchill declared that he supported the use of
the A-bomb. It had, he pointed out, prevented the loss of
the lives of a million American servicemen and a quarter of
a million British servicemen. He also said that the revelation
of the terrible secrets of nature should make everybody stop
and think and that everyone should pray that the new
and terrible discovery should be used, not to destroy mankind but for mankind's advancement and prosperity.

So demoralized were the Japanese at the cataclysmic
effect of the new-type bombs that on August 14, 1945, only
five days after the second A-bomb had been dropped, they
surrendered. On September 2 the Japanese forces formally
surrendered to U.S. General Douglas MacArthur, and on
September 12 the Japanese forces in southeast Asia formally
surrendered to Lord Louis Mountbatten.

Winston Churchill had lost an election, but he was
right about the use of the A-bomb, for ghastly though its
effects were, it had saved the lives of untold American and
British servicemen.

18. Winning the Peace

AT THE END OF World War II the British people were in a position similar to that of the Americans at the end of the Civil War. Old standards, beliefs, ideologies, and fetishes had been swept away, and the Britons were facing an unknown future.

The war had been won, but now the British were confronted with a longer and possibly even more difficult task—that of winning the peace in a shattered and confused world that was already changing fast. In 1945 a prominent American said that Britain was morally great, but economically bankrupt, and this bitter tribute was all too true.

At the end of the war, Britain's national debt was three and a half billion pounds sterling, and one billion pounds sterling of her overseas investments had already been sold to pay for the war. One billion pounds sterling would be needed to rebuild the five million homes that had been destroyed by bombing. The housing situation was so acute that 76,000 evacuees had no homes to come back to. A further one billion pounds sterling would have to be spent rebuilding bomb-blasted factories and works and replacing worn-out machinery and rolling stock.

It was a gloomy picture made worse by the fact that the British Empire was crumbling as the mighty Roman Empire had crumbled fifteen centuries before.

As early as 1918, India had been asking for independence, and now Britain's defeat in Burma and Malaya by the Japanese had drastically weakened Britain's political power and prestige in India, where violent and bloody race riots between Hindus and Moslems occurred. At midnight on August 14 to 15, 1947, India became an independent nation, and Britain lost a mighty possession, one which Prime Minister Disraeli had once described as "the brightest jewel in the English crown."

There was trouble in Palestine, where thousands of illegal Jewish immigrants fought bitterly with the British and the Arabs. Unable to maintain peace in Palestine, Britain was forced to hand the problem over to the United Nations in 1948.

Only three years after this, the Persian leader Dr. Mossadegh nationalized the Anglo-Iranian Oil Company, and so Britain lost her oil refineries and oil fields in Persia. This encouraged King Farouk of Egypt to oppose Britain, and their families had to be evacuated from the Suez Canal. There was mob rule in Cairo, where Britons and British property were attacked.

There were also massive problems to be dealt with at home. Millions of men were returning from the armed forces to civilian life, among them tens of thousands of wounded or war-incapacitated men, who would have to be rehabilitated before they could find work. Some servicemen returned to find that the juniors they had left behind in their places of employment were now their seniors and in some cases even their bosses. The younger men in their twenties frequently returned to no jobs at all and added to the numbers of unemployed.

Even nature itself seemed to be determined further to afflict the British people, for in 1947 there came "the year of the great freeze-up." For weeks Britain was in the grip of arctic conditions of a severity beyond the living memory of most. The seas froze solid as far as two miles from the shore; coal mines, shops, factories, and public transport were frozen to a standstill. For weeks people queued in the bitter cold for rations of coal and coke, and they still had to queue for food rations. Because of the shortage of coal and coke, gas supplies were restricted, and electricity was cut off from homes and shops for five hours a day. London endured a blackout reminiscent of the blitz, and two million people were temporarily laid off work. Nor was this all, for in the savage January of that year the national daily press warned that bacon and meat rations would be reduced, beer supplies would have to be halved, and, worst of all, bread would have to be rationed. Bread had not been rationed even in the worst years of the war; unquestionably, in 1947 the people on the British home front were suffering worse than in war time, except that they were not being bombed.

In 1948 the individual weekly rations for an adult were two pints of milk, two loaves of bread, 1s. 6d. (under 50 cents) worth of meat (cut to eight pennyworth in 1949), one and a half ounces of cheese, six ounces of butter and margarine, one ounce of fat, and eight ounces of sugar. Clothes rationing did not end until 1949; milk rationing, until January, 1950; egg rationing until August, 1950; and meat rationing, until 1954.

Britain was feeling the postwar pinch very badly, and

but for General George Marshall, U.S. Secretary of state in 1947, the plight of the British nation generally would have been a desperate one in the years immediately after the war. George Marshall implemented a tremendous "rescue operation" to help not only Britain, but the entire world to recover from the aftereffects of the war. But for Marshall aid, as it became known, Britons' rations of butter, cheese, bacon, and sugar would have been cut by one-third; and there would have been even less meat and eggs. Supplies of gasoline would have been reduced, and the flow of building materials so limited that the postwar building program would have been reduced by 50,000 houses a year. The supply of raw materials for industry would have dwindled, causing the number of unemployed to rise to one and a half million people.

There is an old proverb that says that the darkest hour is before the dawn, and the dawn was close at hand for postwar Britain.

On July 5, 1948, the work of Sir William Beveridge, soon to be Lord Beveridge, came to completion, and the welfare state, planned during the war, came into being. The national daily press told the world that a new Britain had been born. From this time on, pregnant mothers would receive free prenatal and postnatal treatment. Britons would receive free care and medical services from birth, during their childhood and school years, during periods of unemployment, and in retirement and widowhood. Even burial costs would be taken care of by the state. There would be free medical care and hospitalization, free dentistry and optical services, all for "4 shillings and 11 pence out of your weekly pay packet."

Britain was thus the world's first welfare state. Nor was this all, for important social reforms were also taking place. In 1948 the sentence of flogging for criminals was abolished, and four years later Sydney Silverman, M.P., pressed for the abolition of the death sentence for murder. In 1965 death by hanging was abolished for a trial period of five years, and in 1969 this period was extended indefinitely.

In 1963 there was further reform, for offenders between 17 and 21 were no longer sent to jail but to detention centers instead. Between 1964 and 1965, £7 million were spent on building new jails, open prisons, and psychiatric prisons. Jails also provided films, concerts, and television for inmates.

Britain was progressing on the industrial front also. Postwar Britain played only a small part in the development of rockets and space flight, but she was pioneering the development of commercial aircraft. Newly formed airline companies used British and American military transport planes converted for passenger and freight carrying, manned by ex-RAF pilots and aircrews.

But the piston-engined plane was already obsolete, for as early as 1937 Frank Whittle (later Sir Frank Whittle) had invented the jet engine, and the Gloster, a British jet plane, and the German jet engine M.E. 262 were in operation by the end of the war.

Jet planes gave far greater speed than piston-engined planes, speed that was carrying man into the unknown. In 1946 Geoffrey de Havilland, a British test pilot put his jet plane into a power dive and was the first man to fly through the sound barrier. The plane disintegrated, and de Havilland lost his life, but he had pioneered the way into supersonic flight. In 1947 Captain Charles Yaeger of the USAF, piloting a Bell XS-1 rocket plane, was the first man to achieve successful supersonic flight.

The emphasis was now on the development of jet-powered commercial aircraft, and in 1953 the de Havilland Aircraft Company produced the 500-m.p.h. Comet, the world's first jet-powered airliner. It was a feat described as Britain's greatest technological breakthrough of the century.

But at this early stage in the development of high-flying supersonic aircraft, there was still much man did not understand. Two Comets mysteriously exploded in 1954, one over the island of Elba and the other off the coast of Italy. Forty-four lives were lost. All the Comet planes were immediately grounded; it was found that the disasters had been due to the internal pressure of the aircraft when flying at great height. By the time the defects had been remedied and stronger Comets were in operation, Britain had lost her lead in the production of jet-powered commercial aircraft to America.

Nevertheless, Britain did achieve and maintain supremacy in a new and unique field of commercial travel. In 1955 an electronics engineer named Christopher Cockerell invented the hovercraft. The government, however, regarding the invention from a military aspect, placed it on the "secrets list," and all plans for development and production were stopped. In 1957 there was a change of policy, and the aviation company Saunders Roe was given a contract by the Ministry of Supply to develop Cockerell's invention to a limited degree. In 1959 the hovercraft became a reality when the British Treasury financed the Hovercraft Development Company to go ahead with the project and produce hovercraft for commercial travel. Today hovercraft roar swiftly and continuously across the Channel in curtains of fine spray from the hoverports of Dover and Pegwell Bay near Ramsgate on the coast of Kent.

Postwar Britain saw not only radical changes in air and sea travel, but in rail and road travel also. In 1948 Britain's railways were nationalized, and the famous railway companies such as the Great Western, Great Eastern, North Eastern, Southern, and others were amalgamated into British Railways. Steam locomotives were worn out and obsolete anyway and were replaced by diesel and electric locos between 1950 and 1960. Stations were rebuilt, tracks modernized, and signaling changed. Signalmen no longer pulled big steel levers to change the signals; they pressed buttons on electronic "train describers," which presented illuminated diagrams of track sections.

Britain's roads were changing too. As the country recovered from the effects of war and entered into what is known as the affluent society, more people owned automobiles than ever before. Between 1950 and 1960 the number of autos on the road doubled, and between 1960 and 1970 it doubled again. There were more cars than the roads could adequately cope with, and in 1959 the M1, first of Britain's motorways, was completed, a six-lane, dual carriageway motorway covering the 60 miles between London and Birmingham.

In the meantime, a social revolution was in progress. Women who had earned good wages in war production were no longer content to stay at home. A far better standard of living could be achieved if wives worked as well as their husbands. More than this, the women had been demanding "equal pay for equal work" with men since the war ended. In 1955 Britain's women teachers were the first to achieve this goal.

Women were challenging men not only in their work, but also in politics. Postwar Britain saw the emergence of

Mrs. Barbara Castle of the Labour party, who eventually became minister of employment and productivity in 1969.

But most of all, postwar Britain will be remembered for the emergence of youth, which made itself felt as never before in the whole history of the country. Thanks to free cod-liver oil, free orange juice, free milk, extra rations, and a general concern with their welfare during the war, the postwar youngsters of Britain generally enjoyed better health and physique than their parents of World War I, who had received no such benefits. The young people were also more mature than their parents, for they reached puberty six months earlier. So mature were they, in fact, that in 1964 Harold Wilson's Labour Government reduced the voting age from 21 to 18.

In addition, British teen-agers had more money to spend than at any time in history. In 1959 Britain's five million teen-agers spent something like £830 million, and it was natural that their tastes were catered to by song-writers, book writers, the press, clothes designers, entrepreneurs, and others. This was the age of Mary Quant, who specialized in designing clothes for young people, and the age of the Beatles and the Pop groups that followed them.

Postwar Britain was also the origin of many teen-age cults: the Edwardian-attired Teddy Boys; the Skin Heads, with their tight jeans, suspenders, heavy "bovver" (bother, i.e., fighting) boots, and shaven heads; the Mods on motor scooters and the Rockers on heavy motorbikes, who rode in gangs and fought whenever they met; the long-haired, exotically attired hippies; and the dropouts, who rejected society.

The young people were a vigorous, controversial, and contradictory new breed, at times violent and even vandalistic. They showed little respect for tradition and demanded, and took, part in the running of their schools and universities and in political affairs. Their fathers' heroes had been Lord Nelson, Winston Churchill, Field Marshal Montgomery, and other figures of the Establishment. These were rejected for such figures as the Chinese leader Mao and revolutionaries like Fidel Castro and Che Guevara. Britain's new breed of youth cared vigorously and vociferously about the underprivileged and the homeless. They worked tirelessly for Oxfam, the organization that tries to feed and clothe the destitute peoples of underdeveloped nations. They marched and demonstrated on behalf of Shelter, the organization that tries to house the homeless, and joined the homeless "squatters" when they appropriated empty premises and physically opposed the authorities who came to eject them.

The postwar youth of Britain opposed apartheid in South Africa and racism everywhere. Young people vigorously supported CND, the Campaign for Nuclear Disarmament, organized by the philosopher Bertrand Russell in 1961. British students opposed the war in Vietnam, British policy in the Nigerian civil war, and British policy in Northern Ireland.

It was inevitable that the postwar youth of Britain should be criticized by their elders and called troublemakers, longhair louts, and even stronger names. But for all their faults, these young people have an awareness and a tolerance their elders lacked and care about the world they live in and its people.

For such resurgent youth, "There is more day to dawn . . ." as the philosopher Thoreau once wrote.

Additional Reading

Calder, Angus. *The People's War*. Jonathan Cape.

Churchill, Winston S. *The Second World War; An Abridgement of the Six Volumes of "The Second World War."* Boston: Houghton, Mifflin Company, 1959.

Goldsmith-Carter, Georeg. *Looming Lights, A True Story of the Lightships*. London: Constable & Co., Ltd., 1945, 1946.

Mountbatten, Vice Admiral Lord Louis. *Combined Operations: The Official Story of the Commandos*. London: Macmillan & Co., Ltd., 1943.

Moseley, Leonard. *Backs to the Wall*. London: Weidenfeld and Nicolson, 1971.

Murrow, Edward R. *In Search of Light; The Broadcasts of Edward R. Murrow, 1938–1961*. New York: Alfred A. Knopf, 1967.

Scott, Lt. Comdr. Peter. *The Battle of the Narrow Seas*. London: Country Life, Ltd., 1945.

Townsend, Peter. *Duel of Eagles*. New York: Simon and Schuster, Inc., 1971.

Verrier, Antony. *The Bomber Offensive*. London: B. T. Batsford, Ltd., 1968.

Index